Elizabeth W. (Elizabeth Williams) Champney, Elizabeth Williams Champney

Three Vassar Girls in England

A Holiday Excursion of Three College Girls Through the Mother Country

Elizabeth W. (Elizabeth Williams) Champney, Elizabeth Williams Champney

Three Vassar Girls in England

A Holiday Excursion of Three College Girls Through the Mother Country

ISBN/EAN: 9783744760232

Printed in Europe, USA, Canada, Australia, Japan

Cover: Foto ©Andreas Hilbeck / pixelio.de

More available books at **www.hansebooks.com**

THREE VASSAR GIRLS

IN ENGLAND.

A HOLIDAY EXCURSION OF THREE COLLEGE GIRLS THROUGH THE MOTHER COUNTRY.

BY

LIZZIE W. CHAMPNEY,

AUTHOR OF "A NEGLECTED CORNER OF EUROPE," "THREE VASSAR GIRLS ABROAD," ETC

ILLUSTRATED BY "CHAMP,"
AND OTHER DISTINGUISHED ARTISTS.

BOSTON:
ESTES AND LAURIAT,
301-305 WASHINGTON STREET.
1884.

CONTENTS.

		PAGE
I.	PREJUDICE	13
II.	TOM, DICK, AND HARRY	28
III.	THE LAWN PARTY AT CHATSWORTH	44
IV.	MAUD'S SKETCHING TOUR. FIRST BULLETIN:—WORCESTER	61
V.	MAUD'S SKETCHING TOUR. BULLETIN SECOND:—WARWICK AND KENILWORTH	74
VI.	SWEET GIRL GRADUATES	97
VII.	MAUD'S SKETCHING TOUR. BULLETIN THREE:—THE THAMES	113
VIII.	BARBARA'S LOG.—CHIP THE FIRST	139
IX.	MAUD'S SKETCHING TOUR. BULLETIN FOUR:—LONDON	164
X.	BARBARA'S LOG.—CHIP THE SECOND	179
XI.	THE RIGHT KEY	192
XII.	INTERCEPTED LETTERS	213

ILLUSTRATIONS.

	PAGE
Mr. Atchison	14
Haddon Hall	17
Courtyard, Haddon Hall	20
Harry the Harper	21
Miss Featherstonhaugh	22
Dorothy Vernon's Terrace	25
Dick	28
Maud	29
The Dog-cart	30
Grand Old Oaks	31
The Owlet	34
Elizabeth and Essex	37
Tom	40
Worcester Vase	42
Chelsea Vase in the British Museum	43
Shall I Crush Her?	46
Chatsworth	47
Lady Gubbing, 1882	50
Aquarium	51
Lawn-tennis Match	54
Catherine Discussing	57
Farnese Flora	66
Cromwell at the Deathbed of his Daughter	67
Battle of Marston Moor	69
It was John Featherstonhaugh	71
Lady Gubbins, 1810	75
" " 1765	76
Yellowplush behind His Lordship's Chair	77
Fox-hunting	79
Kenilworth Castle	81
On the Road	84
Queen Elizabeth	85
Past Quaint Cottages	87
One of the Towers	88
Warwick Castle	89
Hoary Keep of Kenilworth	93
Shakespeare's Tomb	95
Potting Plants	99
Jim	101
Milton Dictating	103
The Street Locksmith	108
At the Cabin Door	111
Making up the Journal	114
Mary Plighting her Troth	115
Blenheim	119
Picnic at Nuneham	122
Escape of Empress Maud	123
On the Tow-path	126
Swans at Henley	129
Guiding the Rudder	132
Windsor Castle	134
View of Richmond Hill	135
Augustus	141
Isle of Man	142
Bardic Contests at Carnarvon Castle	144
Carnarvon Castle	145
Welsh Peasant	147
In the Mist	148
Pont Aberglaslyn	151
A Talk about Business	155
Raglan Castle	160
Chepstow Castle	161
The Avon at Bristol	163
The Æsthetic Clique	166
Westminster Abbey	169
At the Foundling Hospital	171

ILLUSTRATIONS

	PAGE		PAGE
At the Grosvenor	172	Dolls for the Tinas	195
Doing London in Hansom Style	173	Plymouth	197
Charity Boy	174	Carisbrook Castle	199
Gamin	175	A Surrey Stable	203
The Tower of London	176	A Surrey Cottage	204
Coast between Tintagel and Boscastle	181	A Confidential Conversation	206
		In the Park	211
Botallack Mine	183	Kensington Gardens	215
Cape Cornwall	186	Lincoln Cathedral	219
Land's End	187	In the Dressing-Room	225
Codicil No. 3	189	An English Churchyard	229
Lizard Point	192	Goethe's Promenade, Weimer	235
Rynance Cove	193		

THREE VASSAR GIRLS IN ENGLAND.

THREE VASSAR GIRLS IN ENGLAND.

CHAPTER I.

PREJUDICE.

"AND in spite of all this I do not like the English!"

"Barbara Atchison!"

"You surely do not mean that you do not like your cousins."

"No, I except them. They seem to me almost like Americans; but English people typically and collectively impress me as the most antipathetic,— the most disagreeable on the face of the earth."

"And yet," remarked Cecilia Boylston, the eldest of the three, a dignified girl with a face as pure and clear as her pebble eye-glasses, "you were in raptures a moment ago over this fascinating little country-house, with the ivy clinging to the stepped gables, making such a rich contrast to the red brick, over this cozy alcoved window, with that wonderful view, over all the quaint ways of the household, and the Chippendale furniture. What is it that strikes the false note?"

"Nothing, just here. It is all perfect. Nobody could find fault with Cosietoft or with my good relatives. When I think of how Cousin Acherly Atchison left his business at Manchester and departed forthwith to America to hunt up his unknown cousins, just because a legacy had been left in which we had a share, his conduct seems to me worthy of one of the knights at Arthur's Table Round. Why, most people would have been content with inserting a personal in the *Herald*, and trusting to our never seeing it."

MR. ATCHISON.

"Then," added Maud Van Vechten, — a business-like young woman already sharpening her pencils preparatory to sketching the towers visible in the distance, — "then it was perhaps quite natural that he should insist on taking you back to England with him to visit in this delightful family; but that he should invite Saint and me as well, because we were friends of yours, and happened to be passing through Derbyshire on our way to London, — why, such hospitality wins my heart, not only for Mr. and Mrs. Atchison, but warms it to all their country-people."

"If this were all," replied Barbara, "or if all were like this; but Aunt Atchison is determined that we shall see some society; and presently we shall have to meet the dreadful bores that figure in Trollope's novels, and whom even Dickens and Thackeray could not make entertaining. If we could wander at our own sweet will through this lovely country, with only books to interpret it for us; but no, we must meet stupid people and opinionated people, talking bores and dignified bores, and for uncle and aunt's sake I must try to propitiate all."

"I sympathize with you, Barb," Maud remarked. "The less we see of people the better. If they are disagreeable it is always difficult to shake them off, and if one likes them they make us fritter away our time. Imagine having to spend whole days on afternoon teas, calling, and picnics, when one might be sketching Kenilworth or Warwick Castle!"

"There is to be a grand lawn-party at Chatsworth next week to begin with, which we cannot escape. Cousin Dick is coming up from Oxford to attend it, and even Tom, who scarcely ever leaves his business at the Royal Porcelain works, is to be here. That will be our début, and after that I fear Aunt Atchison will get up some minor festivities on her own account. I besought her not to do so. I told her we were very simple in our tastes, and would much prefer that she should not make a fuss over us. The two quiet days that we have spent in this rambling old house have been more than delightful. I am afraid they are too good to last. Harry is only a boy of sixteen, and a good-natured and endurable young fellow, but I confess that I dread the coming of my older cousins, though we may congratulate ourselves that they cannot stay long. Then think of the fossils of clergymen and dowagers, and old squires, and narrow-minded women that we will have to meet! Their patronage of America will be even worse than their downright rudeness. I think we have an innate prejudice against the English, and they against us. It is as intense and as irrational as our longing to snap torpedoes on Fourth of July, and perhaps the feeling and the custom date back to a common origin."

"I am glad that you recognize the feeling as prejudice," replied Cecilia, familiarly called Saint. "I who was born under the shadow of Bunker Hill have no such vindictive feeling. If I had lived at the time of the Revolution I have no doubt my blood would have been stirred by the reverberations of the great guns; but this popping of crackers and international squibs of criticism seem to me alike childish."

"What I find particularly galling," continued Barbara," is the fact that the English are so supercilious. They fancy that they understand us perfectly, while they have not the remotest conception of what Americans really are."

"I can pardon the arrogance which comes from misconception," remarked Maud; "what I find absolutely incomprehensible is their lack of taste. Do you remember how those English women in Paris used to dress? They were the laughing-stock of the French. Five shades of purple in one costume, and crimson and magenta married most unlovingly in another gown, while a Paisley scarf with a vermilion centre completed the horror."

"I thought the æsthetic craze had put an end to such atrocities."

"Yes, their artists are teaching them new and better ideas, but Oscar Wilde, and Patience, and Du Maurier's caricatures in *Punch* show us to what an extreme they are carrying the new fashion. I am more and more convinced that the English as a nation are utterly tasteless."

Saint laughed merrily. "Girls," she exclaimed, "if any one needs to have their impressions corrected, I am sure you do. I foretell that before we have passed three months in England both of you will dote on the English. I believe that all antagonism comes from imperfect knowledge. What could be kinder than the reception that we have received here? Mrs. Atchison, too, dresses neither in violent purples nor in dirty greens, but in conventional black. We ought to remember also that we are English ourselves, only a few generations removed, and I for one am ready to believe that all English people are agreeable, could we thoroughly know them."

Barbara shook her head doubtfully. "Cousin Acherly admits that English people have wrong notions about American girls, and he does us the compliment to think that acquaintance with us will enlighten some of his benighted neighbors. I do hope that I shall not disappoint him. No fears about you two, but my evil genius will be sure to lead me into some escapade."

"Never fear, Barb," Maud replied, reassuringly, "you couldn't do anything really shocking, no matter how hard you tried. It is rather crushing to think that the reputation of America, and Vassar as well, is at stake in our insignificant persons. But I believe that the

HADDON HALL.

less we think about it the better. If we go straight ahead without deferring to any one's opinion, simply minding our own concerns, I am sure we cannot scandalize any rightly-disposed person, while if we are continually wondering what Mrs. Grundy will say, we will blunder into no end of *faux pas* from sheer self-consciousness. Of one thing I am sincerely thankful, we have no chaperone to be responsible for. I am afraid that when we were in France together we earned the reputation of being rather giddy, simply because my married sister Lilly was the figure-head of the party. We will sail under our own flag this time, and I have no fear that we shall put it to shame."

As they spoke Mrs. Atchison rustled gently into the room. "Luncheon is ready, my dears," she said, pleasantly; "and after that is disposed of, I have ordered the wagonette for a short drive over to Haddon Hall. Our bad weather of yesterday has cleared away, and Harry is impatient to do the honors of the neighborhood."

They were joined at luncheon by Harry and by his tutor, Mr. Ives; 'an uninteresting dyspeptic," Maud has systematically labelled him on the occasion of their first interview.

"What is your impression of the view of Haddon Hall which we obtain from the library?" he asked of Saint.

"It is even more *English* than I had expected," she replied.

The rest laughed merrily.

"Did you think it would be like Boston?" Maud asked.

"I was afraid it would be simply commonplace. So many of the noted places that we saw in Europe might just as well have been in Massachusetts or New York State for any perceptible difference in character. But this is plainly and unmistakably a leaf from the Waverley Novels. It could not be France, or Spain, or America; it is really what it pretends to be, and what is better, it has the appearance of being what it is."

"It is really Haddon Hall," Mrs. Atchison replied; "the old domain of the Avenels, the Vernons, and the Manners'. It is the castle, too, that Sir Walter describes in 'Peveril of the Peak.' This part of Derbyshire is called the Peak, you know."

"I have brought my set of the Waverley Novels with me," Saint confessed, "and intend to interlay it with photographs of castles, abbeys, and other interesting material which I may find in this tour."

COURTYARD, HADDON HALL.

"And I desire to fill my sketch-books before we reach London," said Maud.

"Dorothy Vernon's Terrace," said Mrs. Atchison, rising, "would make a very pretty sketch. And so would the courtyard."

They crossed the Wye, and approached the entrance in the main tower. The battlemented turrets rose grandly over the trees, and Maud could not repress her enthusiasm. "What an interesting old feudal fortress!"

"I beg pardon," replied Mr. Ives; "the Hall hardly deserves to be called *old*, it only dates back to the fifteenth century, when the feudal period had quite passed away. They entered the great hall, adorned with stags' horns, with a gallery for the minstrels running across the end, and then passed on into the once splendid dining-room, whose carved ceiling still retained vestiges of tarnished gilding. Here they amused themselves by tracing the boar's-head, the device of the Vernons', and the peacock, that of the Manners', in the carvings of the fireplace and cornice. Through other interesting apartments hung with arras, they continued their walk into the grand gallery.

"When the family lived here," Harry explained, "they used to give balls in the gallery. It's just your bad luck that you live in this century; you might have had it to say that you had danced on the very floor that Queen Elizabeth tripped it on years ago."

"What is to hinder our dancing now?" asked Barb, "Didn't I hear you practising on the key-bugle last night, Harry?"

"No, that was Mr. Ives, and I don't believe he happens to have it about him, but if a jews-harp will do"—and placing a large one between his teeth he buzzed away with a merry jig, and Barbara, encircling Maud's unwilling waist, whirled her off. No one looked at all shocked, while Aunt Atchison beat time good-humoredly with her fan. Just at the height of the merriment a door opened, and a group of other visitors looked in upon them. Bar-
bara had a swift vision of the scornful face of a tall English girl, who turned away after the first glance with contemptuous dignity.

Aunt Atchison and Saint were standing with their backs to the door, and had not seen the newcomers, but Harry dropped his jews-harp with mock terror. "Now isn't this a go!" he exclaimed, "That was Miss Featherstonhaugh and some of her friends, that she has up from Girton to attend the lawn-party at Chatsworth."

Aunt Atchison looked much annoyed. "How extremely vexatious!" she exclaimed, unguardedly.

"What is it, dear auntie; have we done anything very dreadful?" Barbara asked.

"No, my dear; it was simply amusing, and quite proper; but Miss Featherstonhaugh is one of the persons on whom Mr. Atchison counted on your making a favorable impression. For so young a person, she is considered very learned, having just graduated at Girton College, Cambridge. She is formal in manner, and I fear a trifle opinionated."

"She's a number one prig!" Harry interpolated.

"I see," Barbara mused, in a tone of deep despair. "It is just my evil genius that gives us this unfortunate introduction. I have spoiled everything."

"Why should you care?" Maud inquired, in a business-like way. "If Miss Featherstonhaugh is a person to be prejudiced by such a trifle why she's not worth minding. I've no doubt the Girton girls

MISS FEATHERSTONHAUGH.

waltz and romp when they are alone and unobserved, as we thought we were. I would like to make a study of her face; the *corrugator supercilii* muscles, and the *levator nasi* were called into such beautiful action."

" I don't care a pin-head's weight for Miss Featherstonhaugh *as* Miss Featherstonhaugh," Barbara replied, " but you see Cousin Acherly has made a point of our propitiating her, and after what has happened how can I ever do it."

"Ignore this contretemps," counselled Cecilia, " make her acquaintance, and talk over college matters together. If she's an enthusiastic Girton girl, of course she's interested in the experiment of higher education for woman on our side of the water, and there's a bond of union at the outset."

"She will probably call upon you," remarked Aunt Atchison, " and you will meet her at the lawn-party at Chatsworth. The invitations from the Duchess of Devonshire include all, and to-morrow the boys will come home to attend the festivities, and the county will do its best for you. Do not afflict yourself, dear child, about Miss Featherstonhaugh. I have no doubt that all will end precisely as Miss Cecilia predicts."

They went out upon Dorothy Vernon's terrace, and from it descended into the garden, where the very yews were cut into fantastic boars'-heads and peacocks. "This is where Dorothy Vernon eloped with her lover, John Manners," Aunt Atchison explained. She spoke gayly, and it was perhaps to distract Barbara's mind from the recent unpleasant occurrence that she began the romantic legend of the ancient mansion.

"The King of the Peak, the last of the name of Vernon who owned the castle, had two daughters, Margaret and Dorothy. Margaret was betrothed with her parent's consent to the son of the Earl of Derby; but Dorothy had formed an attachment, for some reason not approved by her father, for young John Manners, son of the Earl of Rutland. On the very night of the marriage of the elder daughter, John Manners, who had been lurking about the place for some days in the disguise of a forester, caused his horses to be brought to the confines of the park, and just when the merriment in the castle was at its height; when the beacons blazed on the turrets, the tables in the great hall groaned with wassail, and the minstrels were playing their gayest wedding march,—Dorothy, stealing out of the banqueting hall, joined her lover at the foot of this terrace."

"It is just the spot for an elopement," remarked Cecilia; "only notice how the trees of the park encroach on the garden. Lover or enemy might approach quite near without detection. I wonder if Tennyson drew from this legend a part of his 'Maud.' The Hall and the Hall garden are here, and the picture of the revelry in the castle—

> "All night have the roses heard
> The flute, violin, bassoon :
> All night has the casement jessamine stirred
> To the dancers dancing in tune."

And so, too,

> "The lily whispers, 'I wait.'"

"Are you quite sure," queried the correct Mr. Ives, "whether the instruments you mention were used at that remote period? It seems to me that a harp would be more probable."

"Or a jews'-harp?" Maud asked, mischievously.

"I think it an instance of very bad *manners*," Barbara added, demurely.

"O, come now," pleaded Harry, "don't begin that sort of thing. There's no end to the bad puns that can be made on the name."

"I remember," added Mrs. Atchison, smilingly, "that my nurse used to impress it on my mind that I must not help myself to the last piece of cake in the basket, for that belonged by right to the Duke of Rutland. It was not until I had attained to years of discretion that I comprehended that the expression 'Leave something for manners,' did not really refer to the feudal rights of our seigneur."

At the death of the King of the Peak Dorothy Vernon's husband was the first of his name to own Haddon Hall, and it has remained ever since in the possession of his descendants."

After lingering a while longer in the garden they returned to the interior of the castle, for Cecilia was anxious to identify the nursery

DOROTHY VERNON'S TERRACE.

with the Gilded Chamber which Scott describes as the play-room of Julia Peveril and little Alice Bridgenorth. There was no trace, however, of the hangings of stamped Spanish leather, representing tilts between the Saracens of Granada and the Spaniards under Ferdinand and Isabella. Mr. Ives scrutinized the wall carefully for the sliding-panel or concealed door into the priest's chamber, where the Countess of Derby, Charlotte de la Tremouille, was said to have been secreted during her flight from the Presbyterians. "I fear," he said, "that it existed only in Sir Walter's imagination."

"Oh! don't destroy my faith in the Waverley Novels," Cecilia besought. "When we were in Granada we made Irving's 'Tales of the Alhambra' our guide-book, and we found the localities absolutely correct. I had determined to let Sir Walter Scott introduce me to England, and I can't afford to lose my confidence in his veracity at the outset."

"But Scott does not pretend that Martindale Castle is a literal picture of Haddon Hall," apologized Mrs. Atchison. "He simply acknowledges that Haddon furnished him his material."

"There is one room, however," replied Cecilia, "which I am sure must be authentic, — the boudoir of the mistress of the mansion, a tapestried chamber with a number of sally-ports. One leading to the family bedroom, another to the 'still-room' and the garden, a third to a little balcony which jutted into the kitchen, from which she could scold the cook, and a fourth to the gallery of the chapel. I have never forgotten the description, for it was so suggestive of the leading employments of a lady of that period."

"There is some authority for that picture," replied Mr. Ives, "for there is a communication between her ladyship's pew in the chapel and the cook's department. She had only to open a scuttle in the wall to ascertain whether the preparation for dinner was keeping pace with the progress of the sermon."

"Dear me," murmured Barbara, "how the spirit's free flight must have been clogged by such telephonic connection with a lower region."

"It needs no telephone from the kitchen to tell me that it is near dinner-time now," remarked Harry, and the party turned reluctantly from the fascinating castle. As they entered the vestibule of Cosietoft, the serving-man presented Mrs. Atchison with several visiting-cards.

"Miss Featherstonhaugh and her friends have called during our absence!" she exclaimed.

"I wonder whether it was before our encounter at the Hall," asked Harry.

"If you please, mum, they only left a few moments ago."

"Then it was their phaeton we caught a glimpse of as we entered the lane," said Barbara; and as the girls mounted the staircase to their own rooms she added, "It's a cut direct. She knew we were at the Hall and hurried over here to make her call while we were away."

Cecilia smiled vaguely. "Miss Featherstonhaugh's brother was more cordial," she remarked, as she passed on to her little bedroom in the tower.

The other girls, who shared the same dainty apartment, turned and looked at each other in wide-eyed surprise. Maud spoke first. "How obtuse in me! It never occurred to me that the name was the same."

"I dare say that it is a very common one," Barbara replied; "there are probably no end of Featherstonhaughs in England. But would it not be a fatality if this should prove to be the same family?"

"Barbara Atchison, if you wish to be impressive, do take those hairpins out of your mouth. There is not the least likelihood that this young lady with the elevated nose is at all related to him."

"I did not notice any resemblance."

"To that good-natured, agreeable Mr. Featherstonhaugh! How absurd."

CHAPTER II.

TOM, DICK, AND HARRY.

THE mustering of the clan Atchison began that night with the arrival of Dick on a late train from Oxford. Breakfast was hardly over before he was out upon the lawn stretching the tennis-net, after which he politely invited the guests of the house to a game. Maud, urging the sketches on which her heart was set, excused herself, and presently her trim figure was seen tripping toward Haddon Hall. Saint too slipped away, begging the privilege of practising some ballads which she had discovered on the music-stand. "Twickenham Ferry" soon floated in clear rich tones through the open casement to the players on the lawn, — for Barbara had accepted her cousin's challenge to a lively skirmish, and, with Harry for umpire, they enjoyed a hand-to-hand encounter.

"Where did you learn our national game?" Dick asked, in some surprise, as Barbara rested at last under the great oak, fanning her flushed face with a racket.

"We have played it at Vassar for three years past," she replied. "It is my favorite exercise, not quite so athletic as base-ball, nor yet so namby-pamby as croquet." Just as they were going in to luncheon a servant rode up with a note for Dick, which that young gentleman evidently considered of grave importance. He explained to them all at table that one of the features of the party at Chatsworth was to be an inter-collegiate lawn-tennis match, it being arranged that representatives of Oxford and Girton were to play against Cambridge and Newnham. "Furthermore," continued Dick, with some little pride, "I am invited to play for Oxford."

"Harry is going to the Rowsley Station at three to meet your father," said Mrs. Atchison; "he can start a little earlier and drop you on the way."

"Have Prince Rupert and Oliver harnessed to the dog-cart in tandem," Dick remarked to Harry, as the latter left the room for the stables. As Mrs. Atchison and the girls passed into the drawing-room Dick detained Barbara a moment. "Will you not ride over with us?" he said; "it is the 'Duke's drive,' one of the loveliest in the county. I can take you as far as Featherstonhaugh Manor, and Harry can play footman; after that he can drive you to the station, and you can bring father back."

MAUD.

Barbara's eye kindled, but a generous impulse restrained her. "Ask Maud," she said, "I shall have plenty of opportunities to see the beauties of the county, but she is going soon to London."

Dick did not at all relish the suggestion. "O, just as you please, but ask her for me then," he said, with great lack of enthusiasm; "I am afraid of her."

Barbara flew into the drawing-room to execute her commission.

"Now what does she mean by washing her hands of a fellow in that style," Dick thought to himself rather sulkily, as he hurried through his toilet. "That Miss Van Vechten in her gray travelling-suit, with her color-box and business-like air, looks like an agent for a commercial house, while I would have been rather proud of driving up to the manor with Cousin Barbara beside me."

As he descended the stairs, he found Maud waiting with the girls, and was somewhat surprised and mollified by the elegant driving-costume of dark green cloth, heavily ornamented with bands of rich embroidery in the same shade. "That's an imported gown," he said to himself, "evidently it was born in Paris." Dick's confidence in his own judgment might have been lowered, and his opinion of American taste rendered more favorable had he known that the dress was made in Poughkeepsie after Maud's own design, and that it had already served one season for drives in Central Park, New York, and in walks in and about Cincinnati. Harry was holding the horses, and Dick handed Maud to her seat. They had hardly started when Mrs. Atchison called to them to stop, and Barbara ran down the drive with Maud's parasol. Then Saint waved her handkerchief from the door, and they were off, past grand old oaks and hunting parks, by river and crag, through the lovely English county. Through the first part of the ride Dick was silent, with the exception of pointing out notable objects on their route; but Maud, who was perfectly at her ease, gathered up the reins of conversation and guided them as she chose. She

THE DOG-CART.

GRAND OLD OAKS.

began with deft inquiries about Oxford and the Taylor Institution, with its Art School and Gallery, endowed and presided over by Ruskin. "What a privilege it must be to attend his lectures," she said.

Dick laughed, as though the idea struck him as absurd in the last degree.

"What will you think of me when I confess that I have never visited the gallery?" he asked.

"I shall be curious to know what your hobby is," she replied, "since it is not art."

"Tom is the artist of the family. My hobby is water," he replied. "I've a row-boat at the university, and you should see the family yacht at Manchester. She's a steam-launch, and we call her the 'Coal-Scuttle.' Father is as fond of yachting as any of us; he always manages to make a cruise at least once a year."

But Maud was no more interested in yachting than Dick had been in art; she had no mind to listen to accounts of regattas; and with much dexterous skirmishing she ascertained his favorite authors, and they settled down to a discussion of Matthew Arnold and Charles Kingsley.

"Kingsley is a real waterman," she said, pleasantly," and now I can guess that your pet novelists are George MacDonald and William Black."[1]

"Yes," he replied, simply, "and the reason I don't care for art is that I've never seen the sea painted yet — as it ought to be, I mean."

Then they drifted back to books again, and Herbert Spencer, Carlyle, Browning, and William Morris were passed in review.

"You and Miss Featherstonhaugh would be prime friends," Dick said, at last. "She is wild over Browning; now I don't pretend to half understand him. They have a Browning Club at Girton, and are as wise as a company of young owls."

Maud laughed heartily. "You have given me an idea for a caricature," she said. "You know every one resembles something in the lower animal creation. Miss Featherstonhaugh's face puzzled me. I know now that it has the owl conformation." They were bowling along very smoothly, and drawing out a pocket sketch-book she outlined a face that was half human, half bird. The round cheeks, widely-staring, surprised eyes, and above all the scornfully elevated, aquiline nose, was so like the appearance of a startled owlet, and yet bore so strong a resemblance to Miss Featherstonhaugh as she looked in upon them at Haddon Hall, that Harry, who was craning his neck from behind, burst into paroxysms of laughter.

Dick, too, though he could not understand the entire merits of the case, laughed in spite of himself, and in this merry mood a sharp turn through an ivy-covered gate-lodge brought them out upon a closely clipped lawn, before a picturesque Queen Anne cottage. At another time the house would have claimed Maud's attention, but just now she noticed with embarrassment that quite a party of ladies and gentlemen were playing tennis close to a high hawthorn hedge which screened them from the observation of passers in the lane. Maud bit her lip as she reflected that they must have heard the laughter of her companions, and would doubtless regard her as a hoydenish and boisterous girl.

Miss Featherstonhaugh stepped forward from the group. Dick sprang to the ground and bowed profoundly, and Maud held the reins while Harry scrambled to her side. Miss Featherstonhaugh said something in a low tone, and Dick turning, introduced her to Maud.

"Will you not join us?" she asked, with what seemed to Maud rather distant politeness.

"You are very kind," Maud replied, "but it is quite impossible;

we have another engagement." She pinched Harry's arm slyly, and he turned the horses toward the gate.

"More like an owl than ever," he remarked, as they passed through.

"Could anything be more unfortunate?" Maud replied, "than our ill-timed mirth? I wish I had shown you that sketch at any other point in our drive. She must think us the most giddy young persons she ever met."

"And all the while you were talking Matthew Arnold and Herbert Spencer."

The rest of the drive to the Rowsley station ran past exquisite views of mountain and valley. They were near the famous Dove Dale, and the scenery partook of its characteristics. They caught glimpses too of the grand old Tors' precipitous crags rising sharply from the Wye that frothed and frolicked at their feet.

Maud had been silent for a few moments, but at length she spoke; "Tell me about these Featherstonhaughs, please; how many of them, and what kind of people are they?"

"There are only three of them left; Mrs. Featherstonhaugh, John, and Miss Gladys, and they are very nice people indeed. Old Squire Featherstonhaugh was a careless sort of man, and made ducks and drakes of their property. When he died he left the estate head and ears in debt to my great-aunt Atchison, who used to know him when she was a girl, and who lent him large sums of money. He always considered it a matter of sentiment, but Aunt Atchison was a shrewd, close-fisted old body, and all her loans were secured by mortgages on the house and grounds, which are almost as pretty a piece of property as our Cosietoft. Squire Featherstonhaugh was hardly buried before she sent in her little claim against the estate. Mrs. Featherstonhaugh is an invalid, and her children were afraid to let her know how badly they were off. John went to Aunt Atchison and told her that it would kill his mother in her delicate state of health to leave the place. Aunt pretended to be very magnanimous, and said she would not foreclose as long as the interest was paid regularly. John had just graduated, and was studying architecture, but he was not quite ready to enter business, and there did not seem to be any opening for him. All of a sudden Lord Gubbins, who was going out to India, offered to take him as his secretary at a good salary. John went, and was able to keep the interest up and support his sister. There is a farm or two along with the manor, so that Mrs. Featherstonhaugh had enough to live on; things went on very smoothly until Lord Gubbins came back from India and John lost his place. It was the year before aunt died. Ill as she was she was very sharp about her money affairs. Father acted as her agent, and it seemed as if she was bent on persecuting that poor family all she could, for she insisted that the interest should be paid regularly. Father said nothing, but found John a building contract down in the south of England somewhere, which he pretended paid the interest. Then aunt died."

"Was not she the relative," Maud asked, "who left the legacy to Barbara and her father?"

"Yes, and she made a nice mess of it, too. She left all her property to father with the exception of Featherstonhaugh Manor, which she bequeathed to her relations in America. You see she was afraid father would be too kind to the Featherstonhaughs, and she hoped these unknown Americans would come over and turn them out of doors. She had never forgiven Squire Featherstonhaugh for slighting her, is what we young ones have made out of it, though who would have wanted to marry such a vindictive old creature as she was I can't imagine. Miss Gladys' mother is a lovely lady, ten times nicer than Aunt Atchison."

"If she wanted to give the family all the trouble she could, why didn't she foreclose the mortgage when it was in her power?"

"I don't know; perhaps she thought they never could rake and

ELIZABETH AND ESSEX.

scrape the interest, and that a lingering, wearing anxiety like that, ending in final defeat, would be a more bitter thing to bear than a sudden blow."

"What a viperous old creature!"

"Wasn't she? Her name was Elizabeth, and I remember a picture I saw once of our maiden queen boxing Essex's ear. It might have been painted from Aunt Atchison. I was always mortally afraid of her."

"Does Barbara know all this?"

"No; father doesn't want her to know it quite yet. I suppose I had no business to blab it to you, but you have such a taking way I did it before I thought."

"Never fear, I'll not tell Barbara."

"Honor bright?"

"Honor bright. I am sure your father has some good reason for keeping the facts to himself for the present.

"He explained to the Colonel (that's Barbara's father) that the property was invested so as to draw a higher rate of interest as it stands than it would be likely to do in any other way, and Colonel Atchison said that it was all Barbara's, he never would touch a penny of it, and father might manage it as he thought fit. So now father has some scheme or other of making Cousin Barbara and Miss Featherstonhaugh friends before the state of affairs is explained to either of them."

"Dear me!" commented Maud, "what a muddle! They have begun by hating each other cordially. If it was Saint now, she is so calm and unbiased,"—— but Maud was suddenly silent, for another feature in the plot suddenly occurred to her, and she asked abruptly, "What did you say had become of the brother?"

"He is doing well down in Kent; has an order to superintend some cathedral restorations, I believe." Just then a fish leaped in a quiet spot where the river crept near the road, and woke the boy's wildwood instincts. The Featherstonhaughs were dropped, and the talk was of trout and salmon fishing.

"We must bring our poles and have a picnic hereabouts before you leave us. There is 'The Peacock,' that every sporting man in the county knows so well. They can grill our fish for us, and we can bring a hamper or two of good things from home."

Maud looked in every direction. "I can't see so much as a peacock's feather," she said.

"It's the inn," Harry laughed, "taverns I believe you call them in America."

"Oh!" from Maud.

"And here is the station; please hold the lines while I go and look for father."

A train from the south approached, stopped, backed, and waited for the Manchester express. A tall, serious-looking young man alighted and approached Maud, apparently recognizing the horses and dogcart. He lifted his hat ceremoniously. "I presume," he said, "that you are my Cousin Barbara."

"I am your cousin's friend, Maud Van Vechten. You have perhaps not heard that Cosietoft has suffered an invasion of American Goths and Vandals?"

"No," he replied, smilingly; "my father gave you quite another character; but I have not explained that I am Tom Atchison, just up from Worcester."

"You will give the family a pleasant surprise, they did not expect you until evening. We came to the station to meet your father."

The train from Manchester whirled in as she spoke, and Maud

was glad to have Mr. Tom Atchison take the reins, for the horses pricked their ears nervously. Harry returned presently with a disappointed air.

"Father has not come. Hillo, Tom, where did you turn up from?"

"From China, of course. Step into the telegraph office, and see whether father has sent a message."

Harry came back presently, with a telegram in his hand. "He will be here in the evening. I can come for him when I go to the Manor after Dick."

The ride back to Cosietoft was an agreeable one. Maud had been desirous of meeting Mr. Tom Atchison since she had heard that he was connected with the most important porcelain works of England. She spent considerable time in decorating china, and having studied the subject in the museums of France and Spain, was prepared to talk intelligently, even with an expert. Mr. Tom Atchison presently found that the young girl beside him had more than a superficial acquaintance with his pet hobby, and they were soon engaged in animated conversation.

"I can understand," said Tom, "that you could easily have acquired your familiarity with the marks of different manufactories from studying collections; but where did you become so wise in glazes and other technical matters?"

"I have experimented a little," she replied, modestly; "I studied with Mr. Volkmar, in New York, and while visiting last summer in Cincinnati, I tried my hand at the pseudo Limoge which they make there. If one has a pet idea, one can pick up odds and ends of information almost everywhere. When we were in Europe two years ago, my spending money always went for china, and I have a rather nice little collection at home. It boasts a Sèvres teacup in Pompadour-rose, half of a genuine Alhambra tile with the old metallic glaze, a sugar-bowl in Rouen faïence, a bit of antique majolica that my sister sent me from Florence, and a few other good things."

"Have you ever seen any of the really fine specimens of our Worcester ware?"

"Yes, the vase at the Patent Office, at Washington, decorated with Asiatic animals. I want to buy some little pieces for myself when I visit Worcester."

"I shall be happy to add a couple of Royal Worcester plates, one old and one modern, to your collection."

"Indeed, you are too good; but there is something else that I would rather you would do for me."

"And what is that?"

"I am more interested in acquiring information than in collecting specimens, and if you will show us over the works, Saint and I can stop at Worcester on our way to London. I will be more than grateful."

"I will do it with pleasure, on condition that you do not decline the plates. But may I ask what practical use you intend to make of all this knowledge? Do you intend to set up a pottery on your own account?"

WORCESTER VASE,
IN THE U. S. PATENT OFFICE AT WASHINGTON.

"Perhaps so. I don't mind telling you that all my art study tends that way. I visited Saint near Boston, one vacation. She has a cousin engaged in the Chelsea manufactory, and I was very much interested in their way of working."

"What — you have transplanted our old Chelsea works, with their imitations of Watteau decoration and other French designs to America?"

"Only the name — the results effected are very different. What I wished to say was this. It may be a very low aim, but I am sure that I can never be a great artist, while I think I have taste and enthusiasm enough to do some good and original work in porcelain. I have decided to make this my special study while at South Kensington, and you can see now why I think it an especial privilege to visit the Royal Works at Worcester."

"The Duke of Devonshire has a fine collection of china at Chatsworth, which I can explain to you to-morrow," was Tom's reply; while he thought to himself, "You are a remarkably sensible girl, and I've no doubt you will succeed in what you attempt."

CHELSEA VASE, IN THE BRITISH MUSEUM.

CHAPTER III.

THE LAWN-PARTY AT CHATSWORTH.

WHEN Maud returned from her drive, she mounted directly to Saint's room, where she was happy to find her alone, busily engaged in copying music. Maud's active mind had conceived a far-reaching scheme, which involved both of the girls, and she was anxious to begin its development. She confided to Saint Harry's information in regard to the legacy, and asked her help.

"I do not know exactly what Mr. Atchison intends to do," she said, "but I can trust him implicitly. Perhaps with his large family, three boys and two daughters (one married to a clergyman, and the other the wife of a scientist in South Africa), he thinks he has no right to allow himself the luxury of leaving the Featherstonhaughs in possession of their home, and secretly making up the legacy to Barbara out of his own pocket. No doubt he has done enough for the family already, and it would be perfectly reasonable if he wished to make the girls friends, and then leave them to compromise matters. At any rate friends they must be, and they have started on the wrong road. I have only made matters worse, and it is you alone, Saint, who can redeem the situation. You are an English type of girl; you must conciliate Miss Featherstonhaugh, and get her to tolerate Barbara."

"I!" exclaimed Saint; "you forget that I have my own reasons for not wishing to see any more of the family."

"Now, Saint, do not be ridiculous; to hear you talk, one would think that John Featherstonhaugh had proposed to you."

"You know that he did nothing of the kind."

"Then there is no occasion for any embarrassment, unless, perhaps, you are vexed with him for not proposing."

"Maud Van Vechten!" Saint's eyes fairly blazed.

"There, don't be angry; let us face the facts sensibly, and see what they amount to. We met Mr. Featherstonhaugh when we were in Spain, as he was on his return from India with Lord Gubbins. He was very kind and polite to us all, and especially to you. He was plain and simple in his manner, a real brotherly kind of young man, and you liked him as well as Barb and I did, until he told you that he had a secret to confide to you some day. Then you took fright at once, and would none of him or his confidences, and we parted without ever ascertaining what this important secret was. Now, what right have you to imagine that it referred in any way to yourself? Perhaps it was something about an important invention with which he intends to electrify the scientific world."

Saint laughed. "It is very possible," she replied.

"Well, then, without any nonsense, you made a pleasant impression on John Featherstonhaugh, and are likely to make a similar one on his sister. Will you not exert yourself for Barb's sake?"

"If I were sure that her brother had never spoken to her of me, and that my ingratiating myself in her good graces would not be misunderstood —— No matter if it is. I shall probably never meet any of the family again. Well, I'll do my best, — for Barbara's sake."

A little later Barbara burst excitedly into the room. "Oh, girls, such news!" she exclaimed. "My hour of triumph has arrived. The Featherstonhaugh is at my gate as an humble suppliant. Dick has just returned from practising lawn-tennis at the Manor. It seems that the young lady from Newnham College, who was to play at the lawn-party, has suddenly been telegraphed for on account of the illness of her mother. This has thrown the inter-collegiate match into confusion, for they know of no other college girl in this vicinity who can play sufficiently well to take her place. It seems that Dick enlarged on my skill in back under-hand strokes, and my 'show' play generally, and also on the fact that I was a Vassar girl, and so eligible to the contest, which last consideration had, perhaps, more to do in my

SHALL I CRUSH HER?

election to the Newnham girl's place than any other. Be that as it may, here comes Dick with a very civil note from Miss Featherstonhaugh, asking me to compete. Now shall I crush her and decline."

"No, no," exclaimed Saint and Maud, unanimously.

"Oh! you'd have me pour coals of fire on her head, and mortify her by beating her at her own national game, and by showing her how cleverly we Americans can play?"

"No, Barb," Maud replied, "it is time we were dressing for dinner; come down to our room and let us talk it over." Scarcely was the door closed upon the two when Maud (as she expressed it mentally) carefully prepared a cartridge for the second division of her double-barrelled plot.

"For Saint's sake, Barb dear, do be nice to Miss Featherstonhaugh. You know her brother was one of the most agreeable men we ever met. He liked Saint, and something may come of it yet, but we must not prejudice his family against Americans."

"Oh, dear! revenge is sweet. I feel like exasperating her to the last degree."

"But you won't?"

"No, I'll be just angelic; but it's all for Saint's sake."

The next day, at an early hour, the family repaired to Chatsworth, where they were graciously received by the Duke and Duchess of Devonshire, whose palatial residence, with its magnificent grounds,

CHATSWORTH.

ranks among the first of the princely domains of England. Considerable time was given to the inspection of the park and gardens. The fountains were in play, and nowhere except at Versailles had the girls seen them excelled. They wandered through the "Orangery" into the Hall of Sculpture, and out again through the mazes of the French garden to the monster conservatory from which the Crystal Palace was modelled, where a superb Victoria Regia filled a huge tank with its immense leaves, and its royal blossoms, ranging in color from pure white through rose to dark purple. Just before the game of tennis was announced, while they were straying through the picture-gallery, they were suddenly confronted by a portly form, while a bluff voice exclaimed, "Is it possible that we have here those extraordinary young women from America?"

"Quite possible," Saint replied, with quiet composure. Lord Gubbins shook hands with each of the girls with much effusion, and presented them to his wife with a flourish of his hand and the explanation, "These, my dear, are the Vassar girls of whom I have so often spoken." Then he led Maud, with her escort, Tom Atchison, into an adjoining apartment to see some tapestries. Saint followed with Lady Gubbins and Mrs. Atchison; but Barbara and Dick excused themselves, as it was time for them to look up their fellow-players. Lady Gubbins belonged to the class to whose taste in dress Maud had expressed her especial antipathy. She was very conservative even in English matters, and proud of her ignorance of everything not English.

"The growth of our provinces is very surprising," she said to Saint. "I think it must be owing to the interest which her Royal Highness the Princess Louise has taken in them. It was very noble of her to go out to such a half-savage country, and of course her influence must have given a great stimulus to American society. We hear so much more about America since she went out. The interest taken in education is truly surprising. The Princess sent over some Winnipeg girls, who were really civilized. One of them played on a cabinet organ in a really creditable manner. If I had not seen them with my own eyes at a soirée given by Lady Algernon Montague, I shouldn't have believed the stories which his lordship

told me of the accomplishments of you Vassar girls. But now I am ready to believe that our wild, aboriginal tribes can be educated almost to any extent."

"My dear Lady Gubbins," Mrs. Atchison replied, politely, "Vassar is not the name of an Indian tribe, but of an institution of learning in the United States."

Lady Gubbins raised her eye-glasses and gazed at Saint, who was blushing violently.

"I thought she had a very fair complexion," she said, musingly, "but education and the force of example do such wonders. They say that since her Royal Highness went out the natives are bleaching their hair. But, my dear, you have the true English physique, quite the Lancashire type, is it not, Mrs. Atchison?"

"Yes, indeed," that lady replied, eagerly. "I remarked to Acherly last evening that if any one was introduced to Miss Boylston, not knowing her to be an American, they would never suspect it."

"I would like to see the experiment tried," Maud exclaimed, turning suddenly. "Saint has not met Miss Featherstonhaugh yet. If they could come together with nothing said about nationality what fun it would be to watch the result. I would enjoy trying it myself, but unfortunately I have already met her."

"I do not think I could manage it," said Mrs. Atchison; "Miss

AQUARIUM.

Featherstonhaugh knows that we have a party of American girls as guests, and would immediately suspect."

"But we know Gladys Featherstonhaugh," suggested Lord Gubbins to his wife; "suppose, my dear, that you undertake to chaperone Miss Boylston for to-day, and we will see whether Gladys is bright enough to see through the ruse. Come, now, I am willing to lay a wager on it."

"Please don't make me the subject of a bet, my lord," Saint replied, wincing slightly.

"Well, we won't put it in that way, but Gladys is a shrewd girl, and a great favorite of mine. If she finds you out without a hint from any one I'll take her to Ascot, and if you succeed in befooling her we'll take you."

"Thank you, my lord," said Saint. "But pray let Miss Featherstonhaugh have the pleasure in any case, for I have never attended races; it is something at which girls in my set in Boston would be quite shocked."

"Not in good form, eh? The Derby perhaps isn't, but the ladies all patronize Ascot races. Where are they all moving to? Ah! a tennis-match on the lawn. My dear, I believe we have reserved seats. We will take Miss Boylston with us and leave her at Cosietoit on her way home."

The parties separated, Maud and the Atchisons finding themselves at quite a distance from Lord and Lady Gubbins. The players were standing in easy attitudes, waiting for the signal for the beginning of the game. Barbara and Miss Featherstonhaugh were conversing affably, but Maud could see that Miss Featherstonhaugh's eyes travelled critically over every detail of Barbara's dress, a very becoming suit, consisting of a dark blue silk Jersey and kilted skirt, admirably adapted to the exercise in hand. Miss Featherstonhaugh's attire was also sensible, but not so tasteful.

The players took their places, and the set opened with nearly equal skill on each side. The two gentlemen were well matched, while Miss Featherstonhaugh's strong and steady play was offset by Barbara's more brilliant exploits. At last the score was declared "games all," or five for each side. Each game was now of the utmost importance. During the first part of the next Barbara plainly had Miss Featherstonhaugh at an advantage, obliging her by oblique drives to race from side to side, until her fine English complexion assumed the color of a peony, and she seemed likely soon to become too much fatigued to continue the game. Suddenly Barbara served two consecutive faults, and the game was declared "vantage" for Miss Featherstonhaugh. It so happened, oddly enough those thought who were familiar with Barbara's skill, that the next and decisive game was also lost through Barbara's play, and in opposition to Dick's advice. The set was over, and Barbara, flushed, and with an extremely satisfied expression for a defeated player, joined the Atchisons.

LAWN-TENNIS MATCH.

"Where is Saint?" she asked of Maud, but her inquiry was lost in Harry's lamentation over the result of the game.

"You played a great deal more cleverly than Miss Featherstonhaugh," he exclaimed. "If it had not been for your ill-luck you would have won the silver racket."

Dick wore a dubious expression. "I cannot understand it," he said. "You were not as docile as usual in taking advice, Cousin Barbara."

Meantime, Lord Gubbins had led Miss Featherstonhaugh up to Saint, who congratulated her upon her victory, as they strolled toward the refreshment-tent. The conversation glided uneventfully among topics not likely to betray Saint's nationality. They spoke of Europe. "You have visited the continent, I presume," said Miss Featherstonhaugh; and then she compared the fountains to those at Versailles. Next, as a regimental band was discoursing from a neighboring pavilion, they touched upon music and found much in common. Saint spoke of the old songs which she had found; and of the fascination which dialect of every kind had for her.

"Then you are not from the North of England?" Miss Featherstonhaugh inquired.

"My home is in Chelsea," Saint replied, flushing slightly, as she thought how improbable it was that Miss Featherstonhaugh had ever heard of this suburb of Boston.

"Have you ever read Edwin Waugh's songs in Lancashire dialect?" Miss Featherstonhaugh inquired; and on Saint's replying in the negative, she offered to lend her some of them set to music.

"You will like 'Owd Pindar,' I think, and 'Mary Link thy Arm i' Mine.' He has a very touching tribute to the violin, too; it always comes to my mind when I hear Joachim play at the Sacred Harmonies. It runs in this way, I think: —

> 'My Uncle Sam's a fiddler; an
> I fain could yer him play
> Fro' set of sun, till winter neet
> Had melted into day;
> For eh, sich glee — sich tenderness
> Through every changin' part,
> It's th' heart that stirs his fiddle,—
> An' his fiddle stirs his heart!'"

"That is delicious," Saint replied. "The violin is my favorite instrument. Have you ever read Mr. Gilder's sonnet to it? These are two lines from it: —

> 'And now one white small note to heaven doth stray,
> And fluttering fall upon the golden strand.'

They seem to me absolutely inspired."

"They are exquisite. But Gilder, Gilder?—" mused Miss Featherstonhaugh. " It is strange that I never heard of him."

"He is an American poet," Saint replied, blushing once more, while Lord Gubbins elevated his eyebrows and smiled provokingly.

"America is really coming to the front," Miss Featherstonhaugh admitted, patronizingly. " My opponent in tennis just now is an American, and quite a pretty girl, is she not, my lord?"

"Uncommonly pretty, on my word. American young ladies have that reputation, you know."

"My brother told me," Miss Featherstonhaugh continued, embarrassing Saint sadly, " that while travelling with you he met a party of American ladies somewhere on the Continent who impressed him very favorably. Do you happen to remember them, sir?"

It was his lordship's turn to redden and fidget. "Aw, yes. Aw, couldn't forget them, you know, they were so very extraordinary."

"May I inquire in what way they were extraordinary?" Saint asked, fearlessly.

"Oh! they were perfectly proper, you know; but they were so uncommonly clever and self-reliant, and yet so very charming that one forgot their very superior education, and treated them just as you would any agreeable lady of your acquaintance."

Miss Featherstonhaugh laughed, good-humoredly. "I insist, my lord, that your portrait is that of an Englishwoman, and not a very

CATHERINE DISCUSSING.

modern one, either. You remember that Catherine Parr was learned enough to discuss theology with Henry VIII., and had tact enough to excuse her abilities to her husband, who was no admirer of learned ladies."

The conversation from this point until the breaking up of the party, was sufficiently commonplace. Lord Gubbins, when he returned Saint to her friends at Cosietoft, expressed himself as dissatisfied. "Gladys has not had a fair chance," he said. "Meeting Miss Boylston in that casual way, it is no wonder that she did not suspect. We must have another trial."

Lady Gubbins, who was really better bred than her appearance would lead one to infer, and who had withal a most hospitable disposition, seconded her husband's wishes.

"Gladys is going back with us for a visit of a few days at Gubbins Park in Warwickshire. Now Miss Boylston must also be of the party. It is on your way to London, and after you have been with us long enough to try our little experiment, Miss Van Vechten must join you, and together we will make up an excursion to Kenilworth and Stratford-upon-Avon."

Mr. and Mrs. Atchison approved heartily of the plan.

"Warwickshire is the most interesting country in England," said Mr. Atchison. "And this will give you an excellent opportunity for seeing it."

"But what will Maud do during the first part of my visit?" Saint asked, hesitatingly.

"She need not leave us so soon," suggested Mrs. Atchison.

"And then you, Saint, do not care for Worcester," Maud added, "while my heart is set on visiting the porcelain works; and Mrs. Atchison has kindly offered to give me a letter to a respectable widow, who keeps a lodging-house in Worcester. I'll stay there a day or two before joining you at Gubbins Hall, and then for London, and work in earnest."

"I shall be wild to know the success of the stratage admitted. "You must write me, Saint, from Warwick me know how the plot progresses."

"I undertake it," Saint replied, "only on condition explain everything just when I choose. I never attemp part before, and I do not think I shall care to keep it up l

"You are not to play a part," Maud insisted. "Be self, and only refrain from flaunting the stars and str Featherstonhaugh's face, and she is sure to like you."

Saint shook her head. "I have my doubts," she said.

CHAPTER IV.

MAUD'S SKETCHING TOUR. FIRST BULLETIN: — WORCESTER.

AFTER the excitement of the lawn-party quiet settled down upon Cosietoft. Tom and Dick returned, respectively, to Worcester and Oxford. Mr. Atchison spent his time chiefly at his mills in Manchester; Saint and Maud were on their way to London, and Barbara was left to her own devices. She was a fine rider, and mounted upon "Prince Rupert," a dashing black horse, with Harry for her escort on "Oliver," a rather hard-mouthed gray-coated animal from Wales, who reminded them in more than one way of the illustrious Cromwell, for whom he was named, the two explored the charming region in every direction. They visited Alton Towers, and rode to Buxton, now a fashionable watering-place, fourteen miles distant, where Mary Queen of Scots was once detained under custody of the Earl of Shrewsbury. She busied herself also with botanical studies, making a collection of British wild-flowers, in long walks and climbs over the "tors" or mountains in which the county abounds. Opposite each flower she wrote in her album some selection written in its praise by one of the English poets. For the daisy, for instance, after long debate, she chose Chaucer's lines: —

> "I am up and walking in the mead,
> To see this flower against the sun spread,
> And when that it is eve I run blithe
> As soon as ever the sun sinketh west,
> To see this flower how it will go to rest
> For fear of night — so hateth she the darkness,
> Her cheer is plainly spread in the brightness."

These late April and early May days were just the season for angling, and Harry instructed her in the manufacture of elaborate artificial flies for the tempting of carp, barbel, chub, and perch. When fly-fishing proved unsuccessful they did not scruple to resort to the dip-net, and when minnows were their only prey Mrs. Atchison had them fried after Isaak Walton's recipe, with cowslip blossoms and yolks of eggs. Many an old weir and mossy mill-race, or willow-shaded lake, lying calm and dark like a Claude Lorraine mirror, many a sunshiny river, glancing and rippling over pebbly shallows, remained in her memory living illustrations of such poems as "Stoddart's Angling Reminiscences." Mr. Atchison never tired of hearing her sing, when he came back wearied from the Manchester mills; there was a joy in the fresh young voice which matched the words: —

> "Sing, sweet thrushes, forth and sing!
> Meet the morn upon the lea;
> Are the emeralds of the spring
> On the angler's trysting tree?
> Tell, sweet thrushes, tell to me,
> Are there no buds on our willow tree?
> Buds and birds on our trysting tree?"

"One morning Mr. Atchison made Barbara a present of a small silver-hasped, chest-shaped writing-desk, inlaid with mother-of-pearl. "I am afraid, my daughter," he said, "that you will be lonely and homesick, now that your young companions have left, and I fancy that I have employment here for many a leisure hour. I heard you say that you had a fancy for antiquarian research, and this box contains the girlhood correspondence of your great-aunt, Elizabeth Atchison. These letters were written in the early part of this century, and a few of them are from people who have since attained to some celebrity. You have a right to own them, and I only trust that they may furnish you some entertainment."

Barbara accepted the gift with delighted anticipations; but it so chanced that her time was so fully employed that she did not immediately examine the contents of the writing-desk.

Soon after the girls left, a letter came from Maud, dated Worcester. Barbara shared it with Mrs. Atchison, who had become much interested in them all.

"WEDNESDAY, 10 P.M.

"DEAR BARB.," Maud wrote,—"Do thank Mrs. Atchison for me, for the kind introduction to Mrs. Cheritree. She made me feel at home at once, though English customs are all so unlike our American ones. I am quite bewildered by the multiplicity of meals: breakfast, lunch, dinner, tea, and supper. However, one is not obliged to attend them all, and can make a selection according to one's convenience.

"For a manufacturing town, Worcester is handsomer than I expected. I have not made any sketches of scenery or architecture as yet, having so far devoted myself to my pet hobby — china. This morning Mr. Tom Atchison showed me over the porcelain works. You can't tell how interesting it was to me. They employ about eight thousand workmen, and I saw antique specimens as well as the elegantly-shaped modern pieces in white and gold which we know so well in America.

"I secured a quantity of photographs, and made some pencil studies, which I enclose. You can forward them to my address at South Kensington. I was chiefly interested in some vases bearing the 'exotic' birds in their ornamentation. Dr. Prime in his 'Pottery and Porcelain' criticises these birds as bearing no resemblance to any living species.

I was sure, however, that I could trace the golden pheasant, the bird of paradise, and some other Asiatic varieties. You will notice that I have sent you pictures of other ware than Worcester. I never had the whole history of English porcelain explained clearly to me before. In a nut-shell it is this: The first manufactures of any importance were at Chelsea and Bow, carried on from 1730 to 1770.

"The Chelsea wares borrowed their ornamentations from the French and from the Chinese, and also produced little figurines; something in the way of the Dresden Shepherdesses, which were also made at Bow. A figure of Flora, modelled by the sculptor Bacon, and executed at Bow, I expect to see at the South Kensington Museum.

"Then came Wedgewood, with his important chemical discoveries, resulting in close imitations of Basaltes and Jasper, discoveries which would hardly have created the sensation they did had they not been utilized by Flaxman's skill, and blossomed in the beautiful reproductions of the antique in cameo. This seems to me an instance when a true artist tried his hand at decoration, without in the least degrading his art.

About the same time the Chelsea manufactory was merged in the Derby, in 1751, the Worcester works sprang into notice, and have ever since maintained their supremacy.

"This may be very dull to you, dear Barb., but to me it is intensely fascinating. I have gained many practical hints, and intend to go right to work as soon as we are settled at South Kensington. Mr. Atchison told me where I could have my china fired, and was of great service to me in various ways. He paid a compliment to my taste, with which I was not over pleased, as it was at the expense of that of Americans generally. He assured me that I had shown discrimination by admiring correct forms, and then said that he had been told that the kind of ornamentation we affected in America was the wining of porcelain jugs and vases with imitation-satin bows and ribbons. He described one horror: a ewer, apparently issuing from a satin bag, shirred and tied with a carelessly-knotted string, which he had seen praised in an American newspaper. I could hardly believe it. It seems to  me that we get credit for all our crudities, while our good, earnest work passes unnoticed. Still, as Saint says, the misunderstanding arises from mutual ignorance, and the more I see of the English the more I respect their sterling qualities.

"The letter you handed me just as I was leaving was from Saint's cousin, who I told you was connected with a new scheme for starting a large manufactory in America. He wants me to send him designs for a dinner-service,—there is to be a competitive exhibition, and considerable sums of money are to be awarded as prizes. I do not care for the lucre, but the glory! and I shall do my best. Enough about porcelain. I am going to-morrow to visit the principal points of interest connected with Cromwell's crowning victory here at Worcester. I think the career of that remarkable man, from the Battle of Marston Moor to the *coup de grace* which he gave Charles in the streets of this old city, is one of the most fascinating of romances. After this victory our sympathies go out for the king in hiding, handed from one trusty subject to another, concealed in various disguises, in the 'Priests' Hole' of the nobleman's hall, among the servants in the kitchen, and the peasants in the cottage. I like to think that though a thousand pounds were offered for his discovery, and so many people knew of his whereabouts, he was not betrayed. I wonder why it is that our interest deserts the successful side, and that we care no more for Cromwell except when we pity him beside the deathbed of his dearly-loved daughter. But those fierce struggles at Marston Moor, Naseby, and at Worcester stir my blood still. Do you remember Macaulay's description of the charge of Cromwell's Ironsides at Naseby? —

FARNESE FLORA.

CROMWELL AT THE DEATHBED OF HIS DAUGHTER.

'They are here! They rush on! We are broken! We are gone
Our left is borne before them like stubble on the blast!
O Lord, put forth Thy might! O Lord, defend the right!
Stand back to back in God's name, and fight it to the last.

'Stout Skippon hath a wound, the centre hath given ground,
Hark! hark! What means the trampling of horsemen on our rear?
Whose banner do I see, boys? 'Tis he, thank God, 'tis he, boys!
Bear up another minute, brave Oliver is here.

'Their heads all stooping low, their points all in a row,
Like a whirlwind on the trees, like a deluge on the dykes,
Our cuirassiers have burst on the ranks of the accurst,
And at a shock have scattered the forest of his pikes.

'Fast, fast the gallants ride, in some safe nook to hide
Their coward heads, predestined to rot on Temple Bar;
And he — he turns, he flies; shame on those cruel eyes
That bore to look on torture, and dare not look on war.'

"I wonder how Saint is enjoying herself, and more especially what kind of an impression she is making on Miss Featherstonhaugh. Heigh-ho! it is growing late and I *must* stop. I will finish this letter to-morrow."

"THURSDAY MORNING.

"I am scribbling for dear life in the station while awaiting the train which is to take me to Saint. This has been an eventful morning. I started out early, intending to visit all the places identified with Cromwell and King Charles. The battle of Worcester was fought for the most part in Perry Wood, about St. Martin's gate, and in the city streets. The cavaliers made their last stand in the old Hall, which ran with the blood of the Scotch and English. There is a curious old record in the city archives: "Paid for pitch and rosin to perfume the hall after the Scots — two shillings."

"In Perry Wood, where the action began, I was shown a tree under which I was told the devil appeared to Cromwell, and promised him the victory.

BATTLE OF MARSTON MOOR.

"I made a sketch of Powick-Old-Bridge, where the battle raged fiercely, and then climbed the grand old cathedral tower from which King Charles is said to have watched the slaughter of his men. I was delighted with the cathedral cloisters, which have been restored in just the right way, the original designs repeated conscientiously, with no frightful mutilations or anachronisms to jar upon an educated taste. I noticed a gentleman sketching here, and I crept just near enough to discover that his work was architectural, and consisted of geometric plans instead of pictorial effects. I was turning away when he suddenly became aware that he was observed and faced about. It was John Featherstonhaugh! Of course there was no backing out then, and we shook hands cordially. He inquired particularly for Saint, and for you, and seemed much pleased to learn that she was with his sister, and you were at the Peak. He hoped that his business engagements would admit of his running home for a vacation during the summer, so you may see him one of these days. He seemed older and more careworn than when we met in Spain. Ask your uncle if it is not possible that he is worried about money affairs. He had a portfolio of drawings with him which he showed me. They were all designs of mediæval restorations. I congratulated him on being

IT WAS JOHN FEATHERSTONHAUGH.

in his element, but he shook his head. "A man should identify himself with his age," he said, "and not waste his life in repeating the masterpieces of bygone times. I want to supply modern needs, and to be useful to my own generation.

"When I asked him how an architect could do this better than by perpetuating beauty, he replied that there were more vital problems to be solved, and explained that this was alarmingly an age of insecurity in building, and that we would be looked upon in future times as ignorant barbarians for allowing ourselves to be burned in droves in theatres and in apartment-houses. He has invented a style of fire-escape which will be ornamental externally, and with which he proposes to decorate the façades of high buildings. It is to be constructed, where expense is not a consideration, of scroll-work of hammered iron in old Dutch and Spanish fashion; and he showed me some designs of balconies, and connecting lattice-work which were simply beautiful. His idea is not only a humane one, but I am positive that there is money in it, or would be in America. He goes from Worcester directly to Oxford, where it is possible that we may meet him again. My train is approaching.

"Hastily,   MAUD."

"And now," exclaimed Barbara, "I am impatient to hear from Saint. I am so curious to know her experiences with Miss Featherstonhaugh."

"We will soon have an opportunity of learning from Gladys herself how your friend Miss Boylston struck her," Miss Atchison replied. "Harry called at the manor this morning, and ascertained that she was expected to return to-morrow. Your uncle thinks we must have a yachting trip in the 'coal-scuttle' as soon as Dick's vacation occurs, and I believe he intends to invite Gladys to accompany us. But what is this acquaintance with John Featherstonhaugh? I did not know that he had ever been in America."

"He was with Lord Gubbins, auntie, when we were in Spain. We were in the same hotel at Granada and other places. He seemed quite pleased with Saint, and was very obliging to all of us."

"And what did your friend, Miss Boylston, think of him?"

"She does not approve of him at all; but she must change her mind, he is so thoroughly good-natured, and has such an honest, trustworthy face, that I don't see how she can help liking him even if he were not so refined and cultivated. Mrs. Atchison assumed a thoughtful expression. "I have known John Featherstonhaugh since he was a baby," she said, "and I know him, too, to be as good as he is agreeable. He is my Tom's particular friend, and I have had every opportunity of observing him. That was just like him.

'To serve the present age,
My calling to fulfil.'

He always was something of a Methodist, in feeling I mean. He has proved himself a good son and brother, and that is the surest guaranty that he will make some one an estimable husband."

CHAPTER V.

Maud's Sketching Tour. Bulletin Second: — Warwick
and Kenilworth.

A FEW days following the receipt of Maud's letter, one arrived from Saint. It was dated, "Oxford," and ran as follows: —

"Beloved Barbara, — As I assured you at the outset, I was not made for guile and deception, and my poor assumption of the English character would have been discovered at once if Miss Featherstonhaugh had been of a less trusting and unsuspicious nature. As it was, the play soon became insupportable to me, and I betrayed myself.

"We left the train at Rugby, where Lord Gubbins' private conveyance was in waiting, and drove across the country to Coventry. I cannot say much for the beauty of the drive, for one of those ever-to-be-expected April showers overtook us, and it was necessary to have the carriage-top put up. I was a little nervous from the start, at finding myself in such close quarters with Miss Featherstonhaugh, but really we progressed remarkably well. She had an idea that I was educated on the continent, and this served to excuse my ignorance of many English matters. I was careful, too, to observe due discretion, and to let her take the lead in conversation. At Rugby we had only a peep, through the driving rain, at the school which Dr. Arnold and Tom Brown have made so celebrated. I could not help thinking, as we made our entry into Coventry that if the weather, at the time Lady Godiva made her famous ride, at all resembled what we were enduring, the hard-hearted earl might have allowed her a waterproof, or at least an umbrella. By the way, they all call waterproofs 'mackintoshes,' and canes are 'walking-sticks.' I nearly exposed my Yankee origin by referring to his lordship's cane. He crushed me with 'I'm not a tutor, you know.' It seems that rattans,

Lady Gubbins 1810

used for flogging, are the only articles which they call canes. We had considerable amusement discussing the term 'sending a person to Coventry'; which signifies 'declining further conversation,' or 'cutting another's acquaintance.' I had my own private opinion that

I might wish the trip to Miss Featherstonhaugh, before our visit was over. We lunched at the 'King's Head,' and visited the Guildhall, with its fine carved roof, its tapestry, and armor. Then, the rain still pouring, we continued the journey to Gubbins Hall, a rather modern structure, in the midst of a beautiful old park. The mansion is older than it appears, and, among other interesting apartments, contains a private picture-gallery, with portraits by Gainsborough, and other artists of less note, of all the different Lords and Ladies Gubbins, from the time that the illustrious name received its patent of nobility. Some of the old-fashioned dresses were very comical. I would like to see Miss Featherstonhaugh in the costume of a Lady Gubbins of 1810. If you get up any tableaux at the Peak, try to persuade her to take that character.

N. B. — You will need a feather-duster or so for the coiffure.

"As we entered the house, Lady Gubbins remarked that we would hardly have time to dress for dinner. I confess that I was a little disheartened, as I saw Miss Featherstonhaugh's boxes carried up-stairs, and remembered that my trunk had been sent on to London, and that I had only brought a large bag. However, that handbag can do wonders, as you know, and once in the privacy of my own apartment, the services of Lady Gubbins' maid declined, and my cloth pelisse laid aside, I took out my whisk-broom, and carefully brushed my faithful black silk. Then a bath freshened my spirits, and with my hair newly arranged with the silver stiletto, and the linked collar of silver medallions that Mrs. Arnold sent me from Florence, and the fichu of black Spanish lace that you bought for me at Madrid, fastened at the waist with a bunch of fresh jonquilles, which I found upon my dressing-table, my spirits rose to the occasion, and I buttoned on my adjustable train, and drew my lace mits over my elbows, with the feeling that Miss Featherstonhaugh might do her worst. The dinner was very formal, with 'Yellowplush' behind 'his lordship's' chair; and two hours spent at table, though there were no guests other than ourselves. After dinner we retired to the drawing-room, and Miss Featherstonhaugh and I played and sang alternately. She wore an India-muslin, with pale-blue trimmings, and looked glacial. She played selections from Handel, her favorite composer. I find that nearly all the English people whom I have met think that the 'Messiah' is the grandest composition ever written, and that nothing worthy of being called music has been produced since. I sang

YELLOWPLUSH BEHIND HIS LORDSHIP'S CHAIR.

'Now the Shades are Falling,' from Franz, which Lady Gubbins had never heard, though she has evidently been in society sufficiently to be familiar with an ordinary *repertoire*. Miss Featherstonhaugh then replied with two or three of the songs without words, evidently feeling that they were something quite new. They carried me back to the music-rooms at Vassar, and I remembered how I nearly came to hate them from hearing them practised day after day, on every side, with every degree of exactitude and inexactitude. Then they insisted on my taking the piano-stool again, and I gave them a bit from Wagner and one from Liszt. I could see that nobody cared for either selection. Miss Featherstonhaugh admitted that both composers were liked on the continent, and that English people who spent much time in Switzerland very generally grew to like Liszt. So you see that we did not agree at all, and yet, we each knew enough to respect the other's opinion; and through all, Barb., dear, I had an absurd feeling of how very alike we were. We were each of us a bit afraid of the other, and yet fully conscious of our own excellencies; we were outwardly constrained and dignified and inwardly timid. We touched upon poetry, and there we got along better, for Herrick, Motherwell, George Herbert, Shelley, and Keats are prime favorites with us both. Of moderns, she cares most for Edwin Arnold, and— *Bryant!*

"At the breakfast-table Lord Gubbins proposed that we should take a look at the stables, and regretted that it was not the hunting season or we should certainly have had a meet.

"'Do you hunt?' Miss Featherstonhaugh asked, looking directly at me.

"'Oh, no indeed,' I exclaimed. 'I am a member of the Society for the Prevention of Cruelty to Animals.'

"'Yes?' she replied, in a doubtful way. 'Well, it does not seem quite fair, so many men, horses, and hounds, pitted against one fox, and to have the earth-stopper go around while the creature is out feeding, and close up every one of his holes, so that he may not be able to run to earth, is like engaging treachery to help the stronger side, which is quite at variance with our old English ideas of fair play.'

"'We do even worse things than that, you know,' Lord Gubbins added. 'My game-keeper bags as many foxes as he can during the season, so as to have two or three on hand whenever we have a mind for a hunt, then all we have to do is to have one let out behind a hedge, while the party is mounting, and we are sure of our game. No, it's not fair sport to the fox, but it's sufficiently exciting to the huntsmen and the hounds.'

FOX-HUNTING.

"'And it is a very pretty sight,' Miss Featherstonhaugh added. 'At least, Miss Boylston, you enjoy watching the red-coated riders sweeping along the level ground and leaping the bars, the green-liveried whippers-in, and the spotted hounds in full cry.'

"I was obliged to confess that I had never even witnessed a hunt; whereupon she gave me a wondering stare.

"'Ah! you are city-bred,' she said, at last. 'Now, in the country, we are like the Ephesians, entirely given over to the worship of Diana, goddess of hunting.'

"'Did you ever read an article by Charles Dudley Warner?' I asked (for I was so warmed up by the subject under discussion, that I entirely forgot the part I was to play), on 'Hunting, from the Deer's standpoint?'

"'No,' she replied. 'Did it appear in Blackwood?'

"'In the "Atlantic," an American magazine,' I replied, with the pleasing consciousness that I had put my foot in it once more. My embarrassment was somewhat covered, however, by our rising from table and preparing for the visit to the stables.

"I cared very little for the horses, but the walk which followed across the park was delightful. The hawthorn was in blossom, and the air was filled with its delicious fragrance. The hedges, the grass, and the trees were all washed fresh by the recent rain, and the sunshine flashed brightly on the white swans swimming in a little lake. Lady Gubbins said she had heard a nightingale the evening before, and other birds were flying briskly about. I happened to mention Shakspeare's lines—

"'The lark that tirra lirra chants,
With hey! with hey! the thrush and the jay.'

"'How fond he was of flowers, too,' Miss Featherstonhaugh remarked. 'I wonder how many of his favorites we shall find in bloom during the excursion which we are to make to Stratford-upon-Avon.'

"At luncheon Lord Gubbins ordered out the carriage. 'I shall drive to the station to meet an American young lady,' he said, ' who is to join us in our expedition to-morrow to Kenilworth, Warwick, and Stratford; and if you young ladies would enjoy a drive this afternoon I would be happy to have you accompany me.'

"We each accepted, and then Miss Featherstonhaugh asked if the expected guest was by any chance the niece of Mr. Acherly Atchison, with whom she had played tennis, at Chatsworth. On being

KENILWORTH CASTLE.

told that she was only a friend of hers, Miss Featherstonhaugh, much to my surprise, sang your praises.

"'That Miss Atchison strikes me,' she said, 'as a most delightful young person. I was prejudiced against her, but she has quite won my heart. Do you know, I really believe she gave me that game? She was a very clever player, and her behavior impressed me most favorably.'

"When Maud arrived, Lord Gubbins introduced her to Miss Featherstonhaugh, but remarked: 'I believe you have already met Miss Boylston.'

"'At Chatsworth,' Maud replied, with a demure little twinkle.

"But I was getting weary of the constant strain, and longed for some opportunity of disclosure. It came with our excursion of yesterday, which was one of the most interesting experiences of my life. We drove first to Kenilworth Castle, where Maud made a sketch, while we rambled. I had carried Walter Scott's Kenilworth with me, but it was very difficult to recognize localities, though Lord Gubbins was quite positive as to the former position of the 'Tilt Yard,' the 'Gallery Tower,' the 'Pleasance,' the 'Sally-port,' and the 'Great Gatehouse.' I looked in vain for traces of 'Mervyn's Tower,' in which the unfortunate Amy Robsart took refuge during her husband's reception to Queen Elizabeth. We read Robert Laneham's curious description of the merrymakings on this occasion, and tried to realize the scene with the maskers, the floating pageants on the lake, the din of the buffoons and minstrels, mingling with sounds of revelry, and the glare of hundreds of waxen torches upon the entry of the magnificent cavalcade of courtiers, led by the Queen, her powdered hair, her ruff, her brocade petticoat, and even her satin shoes blazing with jewels; while Leicester, her host, the handsomest and wickedest man in England, 'glittered at her side like a golden image, with jewels and cloth-of-gold.'

"If my researches as an antiquary were crowned with but indifferent success, Maud had a charming field, for a more poetic ruin I have never seen.

"'The hoary keep of Kenilworth,
How mournfully and drear,
Its turrets from the crumbling mass,
Their broken forms uprear.

"'The summits crowned with verdure green,
The wild moss creeping o'er,
Where floating in emblazoned sheen
The banner waved of yore.'

"It is only five miles from Kenilworth to Warwick, but the route abounds in so many picturesque views that Maud was constantly urging us to stop and let her sketch 'this little bit.' I noticed a number of inns with such antiquated names as 'Rose and Crown,' 'The King's Arms,' 'The Spotted Dog,' and the 'Mermaid.'

"Near Warwick we turned to our left and followed an avenue of Scotch firs which led us to Guy's Cliff, the country seat of Lord Percy. The story of Earl Guy of Warwick is worthy of being added to the legends of Arthur's Table Round. It is said that 'Felys the Fayre,' who finally married this famous warrior Guy, in his wooing 'caused him, for her sake, to put himself in many greate distresses, dangers, and perils. . . . When they were wedded but a little season, considering what he had done for a woman's sake, Sir Guy thought

ON THE ROAD.

QUEEN ELIZABETH.

to besset the other part of his lyf for Goddis' sake, and departed from her to her great hevynes, fighting menye greate Battells,' espousing always the cause of the injured party. At last, ' unknown savinge to the kinge only,' he retired as a hermit to this cliff, repairing daily to the Castle of Warwick to receive alms of his lady.

PAST QUAINT COTTAGES.

Only on his deathbed did he make himself known to her by sending her a ring. The legend adds that the countess survived him but a fortnight, and that they were both buried together.

"From Guy's Cliff we hurried on to Warwick Castle, for it is closed to visitors after four in the afternoon. We were fortunate in having an hour in which to explore its treasures. Maud could hardly be persuaded to enter, she was so intent on transferring one of the picturesque towers to her sketch-book. Although the castle has suffered severely by fire, it is still wonderfully rich in art and in costly furniture. The Vandycks especially excited Maud's enthusiasm, and I found the work of Rubens and of Sir Joshua Reynolds extremely interesting. Next to the pictures we both voted the old armor most fascinating.

"After our visit at Warwick Castle we drove on for eight miles past quaint cottages, and charming vistas, to Stratford-upon-Avon, where we spent the night at the 'Red Horse,' the inn where Irving lodged. In the evening we adjourned to Irving's room, and there read aloud his charming description of his stay here; and Miss Featherstonhaugh admitted that America had produced at least two prose writers, — Irving and Hawthorne.

ONE OF THE TOWERS

"It was here that I threw off the mask of a conspirator and came out in my true character as an American citizen. There was an old piano in the inn-parlor, and though it was wretchedly out of tune, Lady Gubbins insisted that Miss Featherstonhaugh and I should sing something suggested by our late visit to Warwick. Miss Featherstonhaugh gave us 'The Mistletoe Hung on the Castle Wall,' and I sang "'Mid Pleasures and Palaces.'

"'That song is to Americans what "Annie Laurie" is to us English,' Miss Featherstonhaugh remarked. 'I remember that my brother told me he should never forget the thrill which he once experienced on

WARWICK CASTLE.

aring "Annie Laurie" sung in a foreign land. I believe it happened
Spain when he was returning from India with you. Lord Gubbins
,d he ascertained afterward that the singer was one of the party of
merican girls of whom I spoke to you, and in whose description he
as far more than extravagant. He said that they were girlishly
thusiastic; but then it was an enthusiasm schooled by a study of
e liberal arts to critical appreciation, and not mere indiscriminate
sh. And it struck him as such a pleasant thing that their superior
vantages had not destroyed the capacity for admiration, but enabled
em to express it the more frankly from the quiet conviction that
ey were capable of recognizing a good thing.'

"Lord Gubbins laughed at this speech until he fairly choked, and
could stand it no longer. 'Miss Featherstonhaugh,' I said, 'I feel
ke a culprit for permitting you to say so much, as I was probably
ie of the American girls of whom your brother spoke.'

"You should have seen her expression. 'Impossible!' she ex-
aimed. 'You are not in the least American, you have every Eng-
sh characteristic.'

"'Come, now, Gladys,' Lady Gubbins asked, good-naturedly,
You don't mean to say you have not suspected for some time
ıst?'

"'Not in the least; and you said you lived in Chelsea.'

"'So I do,' I replied, 'Chelsea, Massachusetts, one of the suburbs
Boston.'

"Then Lord Gubbins burst into a hearty fit of laughter. 'Ah!
ladys,' he said, 'you have lost the Ascot. I vowed to take you to
e races if you guessed our little game, but you are not so clever as
thought you.'

"She looked more and more bewildered. 'I have said dreadful
ings about America, I daresay, but you ought to forgive me under
e circumstances.' Of course I told her that she had only been too
mplimentary, and we shook hands as good friends, though I do not

believe in her heart of hearts she quite forgave me, or that she admires me at all as I do her. Really she belongs to a fine type of woman, a little bit out of the world, and with a pure, high scorn of society inanities, yet highly bred, and in her way as conventional as is possible for a charitably-intentioned woman to be. She commands my highest respect, but I believe that you would get along with her better than I. And though our experiment has been a success in the way of proving to her that American girls are not so very unlike their English cousins, I am positive that her heart has not been in the least interested by the specimen under her consideration.

"Our last day together was spent very pleasantly. Early in the morning we visited Shakspeare's birthplace. I send you some flowers from the garden for your collection — daffodils and violets, with sprigs of fennel and rosemary. You can easily match them with selections from his plays. We rode over to Shottery, and Maud made a drawing of Ann Hathaway's Cottage. We stood inside the huge, old-fashioned fireplace, and caught a glimpse of the sky through the broad-throated chimney, and rested ourselves on the settle where William and Ann must have often sat hand in hand in their wooing time. We made a short call too at Charlecote Park, where Lord Gubbins insisted Shakspeare never poached. Evidently a poach conveys to his mind only the most vulgar of ideas. Our next visit was to the church containing Shakspeare's tomb, with the inscription which has frightened so many a resurrectionist: —

> "Good friend, for Jesus' sake forbeare,
> To dig the dust enclosed here.
> Blessed be he that spares these stones,
> And curst be he that moves my bones!"

"Lastly, we paid our respects to the new Shakspeare Memorial Theatre, and we could not help regretting that we could not stop long enough to see here a representation of one of his plays. After our return to the hotel I sang two or three of the Shakspearian songs

HOARY KEEP OF KENILWORTH.

which Schubert has set to music, — 'Who is Sylvia,' and 'Where the Bee Sucks.' Then came an early dinner, and our kind friends bade us

SHAKSPEARE'S TOMB.

bon voyage at the station, where Maud and I took the afternoon train for Oxford, our brains buzzing with all we had seen and enjoyed.

"Mr. Dick Atchison called on us this evening, and to-morrow

he is to show us over the colleges. And you at the Peak, what are you doing, and whom are you making happy with your merry, sunshiny ways? I am impatient to get to South Kensington, where I expect to find a long letter with a full description of your delightful country life.   Ever devotedly yours,

"Cecilia."

"And at Oxford," Barbara mused, "though she does not know it, she will probably meet John Featherstonhaugh."

CHAPTER VI.

SWEET GIRL GRADUATES.

MISS FEATHERSTONHAUGH had returned to the manor, and Barbara set out one pleasant afternoon to call upon her. Harry had offered to drive her over, but she was in the mood for a long walk, and she declined his invitation. The sky was never bluer or the landscape more lovely; her friends had grown kinder, if possible, and new and pleasant occupations and amusements were continually suggesting themselves, but Barbara was out of sorts. It was the old question which would keep coming up. Surely her beautiful life with all its privileges and opportunities was not given her simply for her own entertainment; how then could she turn it to account? It was the hymn which John Featherstonhaugh had chosen for the rule of his life which had brought the question to light once more:—

> "To serve the present age,
> My calling to fulfil,
> O may it all my powers engage,
> To do the Master's will."

What was to be her calling? Not music, like Saint, or art with Maud; she had no specialty. "I wish I had been more of a 'dig' at college," she said to herself, "and yet I always stood fairly in my classes, particularly in mechanics. If I had been a boy I would have finished off at the Institute of Technology, and perhaps have turned out an inventor, but as it is what's the use? There is no need of my doing anything. Maud is always talking about being independent, and the pleasure there is in being able to stand alone. Now it seems to me absurd to stand when one has a chance to sit, and people are always politely shoving out easy-chairs to me." Still Barbara was not satisfied; she remembered the great peace that had come to her like a benediction that memorable day in Portugal, when she had resolved to trust her future implicitly in God's hands, striving only to do His will. There it was again, "To *do* the Master's will.." What did He want her to do? Superior advantages imposed more of responsibility; what could she do with her education? "I will notice sharply what Miss Featherstonhaugh is doing with hers," she said to herself. "Perhaps I shall gain a hint."

As she opened the wrought-iron gate a little bell jingled, but there was no one in the gate-lodge to notice the summons, and looking across the lawn she saw Miss Featherstonhaugh kneeling beside a bed of bulbs, busily engaged in potting plants with the assistance of a tall, stoop-shouldered boy. She arose as Barbara approached, and drawing off her garden gloves shook hands cordially.

"Do let me take a trowel and assist you," Barbara exclaimed, "it is so long since I have played with fresh earth."

"You will soil your gown," Gladys objected.

"I can keep it out of the way," Barbara replied, "and as for my hands, if you only knew how delightful it seems to me to pinch the moist mold you would not be surprised if you saw me making little mud pies."

They worked together for some time, chatting merrily about the flowers. The boy joined in the conversation with the freedom of a privileged favorite, and showed a knowledge of plants which would not have shamed a professional gardener. He removed the pots as soon as they were filled to a donkey-cart which stood in the driveway. "Jim will drive with them to Buxton to-night," Gladys explained, "and will sell them at the market early in the morning."

"Do you raise many flowers for the market?" Barbara asked.

POTTING PLANTS.

"Jim does; he is my gardener, and has certain perquisites of his own in the way of trade. He has earned enough to purchase his donkey and cart, and is doing quite a thriving business."

"He looks like a bright boy."

"He is a born naturalist," Gladys explained, as they walked together toward the house, having finished the work of transplanting. "I found him in your uncle's cotton-mill at Manchester. Your uncle

told me that he was dying of consumption, and hoped I could find him a home at one of our farms for a little while, he did not think it could be for long at most. I placed him in the care of our Abram, man-of-all-work at the lodge, and he began to pick up at once. Abram cares more for the stable than the garden, and he set Jim to work upon the flower-beds. I worked with him from time to time, when I saw what a passion the boy had for flowers, and lately I have been giving him lessons in botany. Really I think he will make a specialist. I must show you his fernery. He has propagated choice varieties for the head gardener at Chatsworth, and has received a prize at one of our country fairs. The boy seems hungry for knowledge, and it is a real pleasure to teach him."

"How good you are!" Barbara exclaimed softly, keen admiration shining in her eyes.

"Oh! as for that matter," replied the other, brusquely, "I fancy it is all pure selfishness; there is no pleasure like it. An education would be hardly worth the trouble of acquiring if it were to benefit only one's self."

"Is there much need for charitable work hereabouts!" Barbara inquired, timidly, "everybody looks so comfortable and neat that at first glance there seems very little to be done."

"If you knew the poor as I do," Miss Featherstonhaugh replied; "I am on the visiting committee for an orphan asylum, and I meet such heart-rending cases of destitution. There is a queer little structure down in the glen, half cart, half cabin, which belongs to some strolling players. A woman lies there dying; she will leave a pretty little girl two and a half years old. She is not related to the people with whom she is staying, and they do not care to keep her. I went down to see them, and the mother has given the child up to us, but according to the rules of our institution the child cannot be received until she is an orphan, and so we are all quietly waiting the mother's death; the players a little sullenly, for this forced idleness interferes with their profits; and I heard the man who is the manager of the company complain because the woman did not ' git on faster with her deein.'"

Barbara sighed. "And I noticed their cart as I came along the lane, and thought how picturesque and pretty it looked. Why, I even half envied them the freedom of their nomad life, and fancied that I would enjoy being a gypsy myself. Can't I do something for that poor woman? Send her flowers, or jelly, or money?"

MILTON DICTATING.

Miss Featherstonhaugh shook her head with a pitying smile. "She is beyond all that now," she replied, "and the child will soon be in good hands." "Flowers or jelly!" she thought to herself, "how little the child knows of the wants of the poor; and what do her kindly impulses amount to when she would not brush the hem of her dainty skirts across the sill of their door? I have another scheme," she added aloud, "in which I want to interest you, and which I think you will find more to your taste than work among our paupers. We have a literary society, which meets at my house this evening. I want you to remain, and if you enjoy our proceedings join it. Jim will call at Cosietoft on his way to Buxton, and let Mrs. Atchison know that I have induced you to remain over night."

Barbara was easily persuaded, and she found the society in every respect delightful. The subject for the evening was Milton. Miss Featherstonhaugh read a thoughtful essay, in which she paid an eloquent tribute to the master-poet's "sublimity of imagery, and pomp of sound, as of rolling organs and the outbursting of cathedral choirs." She drew a touching picture of the life of his wife, Mary Powell, and treated his three daughters, Ann, Mary, and Deborah, with more kindness than has been lately dealt them. At the close of the essay other members of the society read selections from "Comus," and "L'Allegro," as contrasting Milton's intense love of moral beauty with his enjoyment of innocent frolic. Barbara was unanimously elected a member of the club, and was invited to prepare a paper for their next meeting on the "Higher Education of Women in America." It seemed to her that she had never passed a more enjoyable evening, and the prospect of telling this circle of cultured English people what their American sisters were doing fired her enthusiasm to the highest pitch. Long after the company had gone she talked over the subject of education with Gladys Featherstonhaugh, drinking in with delight her description of Girton College, the red brick building resembling a French château, two miles from Cambridge, where she had passed her student life. Gladys showed her photographs of her pretty rooms, the walls painted in terra cotta, and tastefully decorated with just such studio ornamentation of peacock feathers, embroidered sunflowers, Japanese umbrellas, vases, pictures, cabinets, and porcelain as she had been accustomed to at Vassar. She was deeply interested in a view of Mary Somerville's mathematical library, with a bust of that gifted woman, and in the museum of Roman relics; and she turned from the photographs to run over Gladys' school-books on the little hanging book-shelves, to see how nearly the Girton course resembled that at Vassar. She had no cause to blush for the comparison. While she glanced curiously at some authors new to her she recognized many old favorites. Here were Mill's "Logic," Spencer's "Data of Ethics," Kant's "Philosophy," Venn's "Logic of Chance," Matthews on "Population," Mill's "Republican Government," Walker's "Money," with rows of small Greek books and paper-covered volumes in various modern languages. Miss Featherstonhaugh was practically strong in mathematics, having stood "eighth wrangler" in the University class, and Barbara's respect for her increased as she explained that examination for this "tripos" consumed six hours daily for nine days, and ranged from differential calculus to optics and spherical astronomy.

It was really very hard to go to bed that night, or to leave the next morning, when Mrs. Featherstonhaugh, the sweet-faced invalid, took her into her son's room, and showed her the very portfolio of photographs of Indian architecture which John Featherstonhaugh had himself shown her in Spain. A row of neatly-drawn and colored dwellings were framed simply, and hung over his desk. "That is the work that John is proudest of," Mrs. Featherstonhaugh explained. "They are some tenement-houses on a new plan which he designed and executed for your uncle's operatives at Manchester. I hear that they are very satisfactory in a sanitary way, as well as convenient and tasteful."

"There he is, serving the present age again," thought Barbara, enviously; "well, perhaps I will be doing a needed work if I endeavor to enlighten these benighted English a little concerning the real state of affairs in America."

She began her essay that afternoon, immediately after her return to Cosietoft, but had only written the sentence, "England and America need only to understand each other better to become firm friends," when she heard the voice of the senior Mr. Atchison in the hall below, and knew that he had come back earlier than was his wont from Manchester. She ran down to chat with him, for they were fond of each other's society. She told him of her visit at Featherstonhaugh Manor, and how she envied Gladys her patronage of Jim.

"Hum," muttered Mr. Atchison, "so you would like just such a *protégé*, — well, you can have him."

"What do you mean?" Barbara asked, her eyes all aglow.

"I mean that there is a clever little fellow in Manchester, in whom I have been interested for some time. He has fallen into trouble lately, and needs a helping hand; if you have a mind to extend it to him, I shall heartily approve."

"But who is he, and what can I do?"

"He is a young locksmith who has had a stall on the street for a year past. He buys second-hand keys from the dust-sifter's yard for a little or nothing, and sells them to persons who have lost or broken theirs. If a key is required for a particular lock, and he has none that will exactly fit, he selects one as near the size as possible, and a little ingenious filing will make it all right. He is so clever that he has won the name of 'Cutery Joe,' and it is his very ingenuity which has brought him into trouble at last. He had a tempting offer to make a key from an impression in soap, and did so, though he knew it was against the law. This key was used for housebreaking, and its manufacture was traced back to Joe. He has been imprisoned, fined, and forbidden to pursue his vocation further. I saw him to-night as I was hurrying to the station. He has been liberated, but tells me that he can find no honest work, and that the thieves have been after him again with offers of several jobs." He told me that he had resolved to appeal to me before accepting their proposal; but that I was his last resort, and he was starving. I gave him a couple of shillings, and told him to call at my counting-house to-morrow."

THE STREET LOCKSMITH.

"Poor fellow, it does seem as if England might utilize his ingenuity in some better way than to let it help burglars. But what can be done?"

"Just this. I can give him an excellent place in the mills if he knew a little more, but the poor boy can scarcely read, and cannot even write his name. I have no doubt Mrs. Atchison's cook can give him sufficient employment in the way of scouring knives, fetching coal, paring potatoes, etc., to pay for his board, and if you are willing to take the time to cram him with his studies I think that by winter he will be sufficiently advanced to be useful to me."

"You dear, kind Cousin Acherly; it will be a boon to both of us. If Harry will donate some of his old text-books, and let us have access to his little laboratory, I will give him something more than the rudiments — he shall have the first principles of mechanics. I was an enthusiastic student, and perhaps teaching will prove to be my forte. If he is to be a machinist, I know just the preparatory training he ought to have."

"Very well, but don't be too theoretic and scientific."

Cutery Joe arrived the next day. Barbara liked his face; it was peaked and sharp, but not bad. He brought his kit of tools with him, and was delighted with the turning-lathe, small forge, and other equipments of Harry's laboratory. Barbara began her tasks as private tutor with such zest that for several days the essay " on Education in America," was quite forgotten. One morning she opened her desk for writing materials, and the sheet of paper with the opening sentence of the essay stared her in the face. "I must go right to work upon it," she thought, "or the time for the regular meeting of the society will fly round, and I will not be prepared." She wrote eagerly hour after hour, quite unmindful of fatigue, for her heart was in the work, — her national pride was touched as well as her love for her Alma Mater. She wanted her audience to understand all the excellences of her beloved Vassar. Quite a pile of manuscript lay on the desk beside her, — it was time to think of drawing the essay to a close, or it would take an unconscionable time in the reading. Just then the maid entered the room and handed her a card, — Miss Featherstonhaugh. She laid aside her pen and ran down to the drawing-room with flushed cheeks. Gladys had been conversing with Mrs. Atchison, and Barbara heard the latter say, "It is really a very sad case. I will go in to Manchester and see if I can get the poor thing admitted to some hospital."

"Who is it?" Barbara asked. "Is it the mother of the little girl of whom you spoke to me?"

"The mother died yesterday," Gladys replied, "and the people came to me at once to have the child taken away; but in this interval the poor little thing has been taken ill with scarlet fever, and the managers of the orphan asylum very properly refuse to receive her for fear of contagion for the other inmates. The people threaten to leave her in a ditch, and have announced their intention of travelling on without her to-morrow morning. I had hoped that Mrs. Atchison might know of some woman who could be induced by good wages to nurse the child until she recovers, when the asylum is ready to receive her."

A pained look crossed Mrs. Atchison's kind face. "I will take her into this house gladly," she said, "if I can induce any of the maids to take care of her."

"Oh! will you, auntie?" Barbara exclaimed, with delight, "then let me nurse the little thing; for once in my life I shall be doing something really useful."

"You!" exclaimed both Mrs. Atchison and Miss Featherstonhaugh, in unanimous surprise.

"Why not, it can't be so very difficult, the doctor will tell me what to do."

"But how about your essay for our club?" asked Miss Featherstonhaugh.

"Oh! that is nearly written, and I daresay I shall have plenty of time to finish it between doses."

"But you can't read it, my dear," explained Mrs. Atchison; "you forget that you will have to be isolated from every one on account of contagion. You would have to remain a prisoner in your own room, with only a solitary walk in the park occasionally by way of diversion. I fear your health will give way, and I do not think I can allow it."

"Nonsense!" exclaimed Barbara. "I am thoroughly well, and equal to any kind of a strain. Of the two things it is a great deal more important that this baby should be taken care of than that the club should enjoy my essay, inestimable privilege though it would doubtless be. Where is the child? Shall I go with you, Miss Featherstonhaugh, — how are we to bring her here?" She spoke gayly, and Gladys could not guess what a trial it was to her to give up the reading.

Mrs. Atchison rang for a servant. "Have the phaeton brought to the door at once," she said; adding to Barbara, "well, my dear, since you are determined upon it, I will not forbid you, only if I see that your health is suffering you must let me interfere. I will see imme-

liately that a cot is placed in your room, and everything shall be
in readiness for the child's reception."

As Barbara flew up-stairs for her hat and wraps she met Joe.
"You poor fellow!" she exclaimed, "must I give up teaching you, I
wonder."

"What's up, Miss?" Joe asked, anxiously.

AT THE CABIN DOOR.

Barbara explained the facts in the case, and Joe replied eagerly.
"I'm in luck, Miss, I've had it. 'Twon't do me no harm to come into
the room and say my lessons. Mebbe I can help you too in nussin'
the little un."

"I don't know about that," Barbara replied; "we must keep as
isolated as possible on account of the family, but perhaps we can
meet for recitation on the upper piazza just outside my window, where
I can watch the child and run to her if she cries."

"I'll drive you over to the shanty," Joe volunteered. "'Taint likely Mrs. Atchison would like to have Master Harry expose hisself; and the coachman would lose his situation first."

Gladys parted from them at the cabin-door. "You must read us your essay when you are out of quarantine," she said, "and meantime I want you to know that I have underestimated you, but I shall do so no longer. You are braver and more unselfish than I could ever be. You are the noblest girl that I have ever known."

CHAPTER VII.

MAUD'S SKETCHING TOUR. BULLETIN THREE: — THE THAMES.

THE days crept slowly by and spring glided into summer. The task which Barbara had imposed upon herself was more wearing than she had imagined. The loneliness, the lack of sleep, and the constant care were a strain under which even her fine physique bent slightly, but she was too proud and too unselfish to complain. She bore up bravely from day to day, amusing her little charge with games and dolls, as after the crisis the peevishness of convalescence took the place of more alarming symptoms. Mrs. Atchison allowed Joe to act as nurse daily for half an hour, so that Barbara could keep up her habit of a walk in the grounds, and the lessons were continued on the verandah roof as Barbara had suggested, while the small patient enjoyed her afternoon nap. These lessons were her only amusement, for Joe progressed rapidly, and was profoundly grateful. Mrs. Atchison prepared tempting little lunches, and Miss Featherstonhaugh sent in books and periodicals, but Barbara found that the double task of nursing and teaching left her too tired to read anything but letters. These came at regular intervals from her father in America, and from Saint and Maud. One arrived from Saint early in Barbara's imprisonment, and we will glance over her shoulder while she reads it.

"ON THE THAMES.

"BELOVED BARBARA, — I am seated in a row-boat and scratching away upon one of Maud's sketching-blocks while we drift evenly and gently down the stream. How I came in just this situation I will leave for further development, as I think a consecutive story is the least confusing, and I believe Maud wrote you last just after our arrival in Oxford.

"We stopped at the Randolph Hotel, which Mr. Atchison recommended, and Dick paid his respects to us early in the evening. The next day he very kindly took us about everywhere,—to Christ Church, Oriel, Merton, and Magdalen Colleges in the morning, and to other places of interest in the afternoon. Magdalen is by far the most interesting to me, although Christ Church is more pretentious architecturally, and its kitchens are very curious. There are some old symbolic images in the Magdalen quadrangle which are funny beyond description. They represent the Virtues and the Vices, and reminded me of the gargoyles we saw at Batalha in Portugal. Dick informed us that his sister, Mrs. Isham, and her reverend husband, were to come to Oxford that afternoon, Mr. Isham to attend some ecclesiastical council, and Mrs. Isham to grace with him a grand dinner at the house of the Canon of something or other. We met her at luncheon; she was very sweet and lovely, and reminded me of her mother; Mr.

MAKING UP THE JOURNAL.

MARY PLIGHTING HER TROTH.

Isham is a jolly, red-faced man, not in the least one's idea of a clergyman. She inquired how long we intended to stay in Oxford, and thought two days entirely too short a time. Dick lamented that we had not waited for Commemoration Week in June, when the place is very gay, and he insisted that we must have a picnic somewhere to try the boating. Then Mrs. Isham proposed a charming plan, which we have since carried out. 'I do not care to remain in Oxford after the dinner,' she said; 'why can't you let me chaperone the young ladies, and we will hire a boat and make a rowing-party down the river to our home. I would enjoy such an outing immensely.' The Ishams live at Great Marlow, about eighteen miles from Windsor, and over fifty from Oxford. This will give us three days on the river, with stops at all sorts of enchanting places and a visit at Mrs. Isham's as a finale. Of course we were delighted at her goodness, and accepted with enthusiasm. Dick said that as Mr. Isham was obliged to remain to the council, and one oarsman was rather a small working crew, he would like to have the privilege of inviting a friend to share the excursion. He informed us that there were some thirty Americans studying at Oxford, and that he knew one, a heretical but bright young man from Chicago, who was one of the Baliol set, whom he thought we would all like. Mrs. Isham gave him *carte blanche*, and of course we had nothing to say.

The afternoon was devoted to more colleges, — Queen's, New College with its lovely gardens, All Souls with its interesting library quadrangle. Brasenose, an actual nose sniffing the air over the entrance, the Bodleian Library, the Martyr's Memorial, erected to Cranmer, Latimer, and Ridley, who were burned here in 1555; the Taylor Institute, with its gallery of paintings, and its original drawings by Raphael and Michael Angelo, and the Observatory in the evening. Saturn with his rings looked just as familiar as the last time he looked in upon us at one of Miss Mitchell's observatory receptions. We had seen a great deal too much for one day; but I think that the Martyrs' Memorial made the deepest impression on my mind. It took me back to the relics of the Inquisition which we saw in Spain, and I dreamed that night that I was wandering in the gloomy labyrinths of the Escorial. There was an odd method in my madness, too, for it was for love of Philip II. of Spain that Queen Mary planted the Inquisition in England. I think her constancy and devotion to that man, from the time that she secretly plighted her troth to him before the Virgin in her private chapel, through the long list of her terrible but conscientious crimes, down to her death, forsaken and broken-hearted, — is one of the most pitiful pages in history.

"Our last day I insisted rather selfishly on driving to Blenheim, the site of Woodstock, and the famous maze in which Henry II. hid Rosamond Clifford from Queen Eleanor. Maud was very sweet in giving up some sketching in Oxford to my mania for following up the Waverley Novels, but I do not think that after it was over she regretted the day, for we had a charming drive in an odd little jaunting-car, with a queer character for a driver, a perfect encyclopædia in the way of local information. There is not a vestige of the original 'Bower.' The place was given by the nation to the Duke of Marlborough, and named for his great victory. He erected a grand palace here, with a rich picture-gallery, and other delights which I cannot begin to describe. The park is ingeniously planted in groups of oaks and cedars to represent the battle of Blenheim, each battalion of soldiers being figured by a distinct plantation of trees. Southey's poem, which I learned when a very little girl, would keep perversely running in my head, and I could not refrain from asking: —

"'But what good came of it at last?' with little Peterkin.

"On our return to Oxford in the evening, a very odd thing happened. Dick Atchison called to say that he had secured another oarsman for our excursion. And of all persons in the world whom do you think it turned out to be? None other than John Featherstonhaugh. It seems that Dick happened to come across him here in

BLENHEIM.

Oxford, that he is on his way to Windsor, and that he accepted very complaisantly the offer of a bench and an oar in our boat. So here we are booked for a three days *tête-à-tête*. If he conducts himself as well as he has done this morning I shall have no cause to complain. So far he has devoted himself very gallantly to Mrs. Isham, and as Maud and Dick are capital friends, I sit in the stern, mind the rudder on occasion, and scribble to you. An opportunity has just occurred to post this letter.

" Hastily,   CECILIA."

The boating-trip down the Thames proved a most delightful experience. The more the girls saw of Mrs. Isham the more they felt themselves drawn to the lovely little lady. Though habitually cheerful and animated, they noticed that when the conversation lagged a pensive shade crossed her face, and she would remain for some time silent and distraught. Dick gave Maud the clew to her melancholy. She had lost a little daughter a year before, and this visit to Oxford had been her first appearance among her friends since the sad event. He hoped that this excursion would do her good, and the party one and all exerted themselves to draw her out of herself.

They had passed a quiet Sunday at Oxford, and had started on their trip so early Monday morning that they breakfasted at Nuneham, a favorite spot for picnics from Oxford, and one of the most enchanting little Edens on the river. They moored their boat close to the bank, and spread their cloth within view of the graceful bridge. Dick had coffee made at one of the cottages, and Mrs. Isham displayed the cold luncheon which she had put up at Oxford. A boy happened along with a cabbage-leaf filled with tempting strawberries, and they ate with appetites sharpened by the early pull down the river. After breakfast they strolled together over the park belonging to the mansion of the Harcourt family, inspecting its tasteful gardens, with their terraces, orangeries, and rosaries, and rambling by many charming cottages. Maud made a hasty sketch of the bridge, and then all embarked for a steady row to Day's Lock, with only a peep at Abingdon on the way. The locks were an interesting feature to the girls, as were the picturesque inns which marked their progress.

PICNIC AT NUNEHAM.

They lunched at the "Barley Mow," and Saint began a list of the suggestive names of riverside hostelries. Slipping under Shillingford Bridge, and cheering their flagging energies with the "Canadian Boat-song," the party drew in their oars at Wallingford, deciding to spend the night at the "Town Arms." After dinner Dick announced his intention of looking up a fisherman of his acquaintance by the name of Cloudesley.

"Is he a descendant of the outlaw of that name?" Maud asked. "Don't you remember, Saint, 'Clim of the Cleugh, and William of Cloudesley,' in the old ballad that Bishop Coxe read us one evening at Vassar?"

"He is so very respectable," Dick replied, "that I fear he would resent the idea.

Dick departed in search of his aquatic acquaintance, and the others followed John Featherstonhaugh's guidance in a visit to the ruins of the castle where the Empress Maud was besieged by King Stephen after her flight from Oxford.

ESCAPE OF EMPRESS MAUD.

"I wonder why it is," Maud asked, "that Dick persisted in calling me Empress Maud after the party at Chatsworth? I was not trying to escape from any one."

"When Maud fled from Oxford," John Featherstonhaugh replied, "it was a winter night, and she had her attendants dressed in white to escape observation as they glided over the snow."

"And I wore white at the lawn-party, but not from fear of any King Stephen."

"Was it not rather to attract the attention of Oxford?" Saint asked, mischievously.

"Now, Saint, that is really malicious. I decline your company home after such unkindness. I am going to escort Mrs. Isham, and leave you to Mr. Featherstonhaugh."

"Is my society to be considered in the light of a penalty?" the young architect asked, as he took his place respectfully by Saint's side.

"Mrs. Van Vechten tells me you have been visiting with my sister; I should like to have your opinion of her."

"It is doubtless higher than hers of me. I was a party to a little trick whose bearings I do not think I entirely realized at the time;" and Saint gave the young man a detailed account of her experiences in Warwickshire.

"Gladys can enjoy a joke even at her own expense," John Featherstonhaugh replied. "I wonder what her impressions of Miss Atchison were. She would hardly have taken her for an English girl."

Saint took this as an aspersion against her friend, and fired up at once. "If she ever really knows Barb," she said, "she will discover that she is worth ten such girls as I am."

John Featherstonhaugh smiled oddly; "It would be hardly polite for me to agree with you," he replied.

The second day they pursued their journey as far as Sonning, making their longest halt at Mapledurham, which Maud agreed had been rightly called a Painter's Paradise. Here they left their boat with the keeper of the lock to be brought on to them at the Roebuck Inn, a mile further down the river. They then hired a wagonette and drove to Hardwicke House, a fine old Tudor mansion, one of the hiding-places of Charles II. Their drive took them past the Mapledurham Mill as well, the most paintable on the river; but when

Maud attempted to use her pencils she found that the rowing in which she had indulged freely the day before had cramped and blistered her hands to such an extent that sketching was out of the question. As they passed the seat of the Blounts John Featherstonhaugh explained the characteristics of the Elizabethan style of architecture, with its broad expanses of windows, letting sheets of light into every apartment. "You must have noticed this peculiarity at the Peak," he said, "and perhaps have heard the couplet, —

"'Haddon Hall
More glass than wall.'"

From the Elizabethan he branched off to a short explanation of the Queen Anne style, and the ride to the Roebuck Inn seemed to all a remarkably short one. They lunched leisurely, for their boat was not in sight; and it was not until Dick had searched vigorously for some time that he discovered that the lock-keeper's shockheaded boy had moored it under the willows, and was calmly fishing for chub. "Don't stop to go snipe-shooting on your way back," was Dick's parting injunction, as he gave the wagonette into the charge of the culprit, and assisted the girls once more into the boat.

"I shall not row again to-day," Maud said, rather ruefully, as she regarded her blistered hands. "I can't afford to lose these lovely views."

"There is no need of any of us taking an oar this afternoon," Dick replied. "There is a good bit of towing as you near Sonning."

"You don't mean to go down in the wake of a steam-launch?"

"Or to engage a boy and horse in canal-boat style?"

"No, indeed; two of us will take a line and run along the parade on the margin of the river. It gives a change of exercise, and is the regular thing which all pleasure-parties do about here."

This was indeed a novel experience. All the length of the tow-path they overtook and were passed by merry parties of young men in gay boating costumes, and young girls, evidently from the best circles of English society, tripping gayly along with their boats in tow; and very often their comfortable mammas seated composedly therein, regarding their lively teams with serene complaisance. While Maud and Dick carried the towing-line together they compared their plans for the future. "I know you won't believe it," Dick said, after listening to Maud for a time, "but I mean to be a worker, too."

"In what line, pray?"

"In father's. I am going to have him start me as a manufacturer, in America."

"In America?"

"Yes, everything is moving that way, and father invested in some land in Alabama when he was over there. There's immense water-power on it, and he means to put up a mill. It is in one of the cotton-producing States, and there are hordes of negroes all around who need employment. I have about persuaded father to let me go over and run the thing for him as soon as I am graduated."

ON THE TOW-PATH.

"The idea quite fires one's imagination, but will it pay?"

"It will pay fast enough if father makes up his mind to undertake it. He is slow and sure. It would kill me to settle down in Manchester, and just grind on in father's footsteps. I want to found an enterprise of my own. Now Tom is a regular conservative, but circumstances lately have led my consideration to the States; they are bound to go ahead of us in the future, and I want to be one of the new movement. All wide-awake men are looking toward America. Gladstone agrees with me."

Maud smiled at the unconscious arrogance with which this assertion was made.

"When did you explain your opinions to Gladstone?" she inquired, demurely.

Dick flushed. "I have gained them in part from him," he confessed. "I had a thesis on America in which I quoted from him largely, and can reel off his very words. He believes that you are going to run us out on manufactures and in commercial pre-eminence. He says, 'America will probably become, what we are now, the head servant in the great household of the world, the employer of all employed, because her service will be the most and ablest. We have no more title against her than Venice, or Genoa, or Holland has had against us.'"

"That is generous I am sure. I have a better opinion of Gladstone than ever before, and that's saying a great deal. But how will Miss Featherstonhaugh enjoy emigrating to America?"

"Gladys? Oh! she and Tom are of one mind; they would both be content to stay in England forever."

"But I thought you admired her especially."

"I'm in duty bound to do so since she is to be my sister some day."

"Is she engaged to your brother Tom?"

"Yes, that was all satisfactorily arranged when they were in pinafores. It is a lingering complaint, and there is no telling just when it will prove fatal, though I believe it is considered quite incurable."

"What hinders their being married at once?"

"Gladys is too good a daughter to take her mother away from the Manor, or to leave her for any long period, and Worcester is rather a longish distance from the Peak. So they have concluded to wait. It's quite the regular way here in England. Jacob and Rachel are nothing in comparison."

While Maud and Dick were on the tow-path Saint sat dreamily at the helm listening to John Featherstonhaugh's pleasant voice as he read from a volume of poems. The finely-modulated cadences seemed to keep time with the soft thud of the waves against the side of the boat, as the current swirled on, reminding her of the "master-poet's" description of the Avon.

> "Giving a gentle kiss to every sedge
> It overtaketh in its pilgrimage."

Mrs. Isham's slender fingers were busy with some gossamer crochet, and a sweet smile lit her face. Sad thoughts had vanished, and her attention was held by the story. Saint could not have told what the poem was, but the picture remained long in her memory — the shimmer of light upon the water, the puffs of cool air playing with Mrs. Isham's beautiful hair, and John Featherstonhaugh's intelligent, manly face.

"There is something in him that I really respect and like," she thought to herself, "if he will only please not like me; and indeed he is doing very well, he is actually endurable."

They put up that night at the "French Horn," and made an early fishing-party the next morning, catching a good basket of trout, barbel, and perch in the lock pools before breakfast. They passed Henley that morning, noted for its swans, its beautiful old church, and for the annual regatta which Charles Reade describes in "Very Hard Cash." The longest halts of the day were made at Medmenham and Bisham Abbey — picturesque old structures in the midst of country filled with charming cottages nearly covered with greenery,

SWANS AT HENLEY.

fascinating moated granges, churches covered with ivy, and suggestive glimpses of village spires over clustering foliage. Just as evening fell they drew in their oars at Marlow Bridge, where Mrs. Isham's phaeton was found awaiting them. Mrs. Isham and the girls drove across to the vicarage, while Dick and John Featherstonhaugh bestowed the boat in proper keeping and followed them on foot. The vicarage had every appearance of being the home of cultivated and happy people, but on entering her own doorway the shadow which had been lifted for a time from Mrs. Isham's face fell once more, and she was unable to join them at dinner. A crayon head of the little child whom she had lost hung over the mantel, and all conversed that evening in more subdued tones. Saint seated herself at the piano and sang a selection from "Jean Ingelow," to which she had herself composed a simple but sympathetic accompaniment: —

> "When I remember something which I had,
> But which is gone, and I must do without,
> I sometimes wonder how I can be glad.
> Even in cowslip-time, when hedges sprout,
> It makes me sigh to think on it, but yet
> My days will not be better days should I forget."

Mrs. Isham, sitting in her darkened room with the door ajar, heard it and was comforted.

They had planned to part here; Dick to return to Oxford, and the girls to continue their journey to London by rail. But John Featherstonhaugh's destination was Windsor, and Dick pleaded so strongly for one more day on the river that the girls relented; and, bidding a regretful farewell to Mrs. Isham, the next day found them once more in their boat. From Marlow to Windsor the scenery increases in loveliness; Cookham, Ray Mead, Cliveden, have all been praised by poet and artist. They left their boat at Maidenhead for a drive to the celebrated Burnham Beeches, — a grove of gnarled and hoary giants which Maud declared were each of them enchanted Druids, stiffened to trees in the act of extending their gaunt arms at one of their mysterious orgies. A brisk row from Maidenhead brought them to Monkey Island, named from a room in this inn, once a pleasure-house of the Duke of Marlborough, and grotesquely frescoed by him with frolicsome monkeys. They progressed during the afternoon chiefly by towing. They passed Windsor, intending to visit Eton and to return in time to dine at the "White Hart," where they would separate. They threaded the border of the royal park, walking through

GUIDING THE RUDDER.

her majesty's private property, where none but persons towing a boat were allowed on shore. They glanced about from time to time, half expecting to meet some member of the royal household, and enlivened the way with the pleasant confidential chat with which friends will fill their last hours together. Maud and Dick talked of America, Maud taking an almost maternal interest in the young man's plans. She thought him very immature, and considered that she was immensely his superior in experience and in knowledge of the world, but for all this he interested her, and she gave him a great deal of valuable information touching the New World, to which he was going.

Was there something confidence-provoking in the clear blue sky and delicious air? Saint and John Featherstonhaugh, in the gently-moving boat, were at the same time conversing without restraint in a frank and friendly fashion, which a few days previous Saint would hardly have thought possible. "He is really a very good fellow," she thought. "I wish he were my brother"; and then he entirely destroyed the good opinion which she had grudgingly granted him by saying:—

"Miss Boylston, I cannot flatter myself that you recollect it, but once in Portugal I was very near telling you a secret which has an important bearing on my life."

Saint stiffened at once, leaned back in her seat, and tightened her grasp on the rudder-ropes. "I wish he would keep his secrets to himself," she thought, and she added aloud, " Secrets are unpleasant things. I really believe we would be better friends if you did not trust me with yours. I might betray it or something."

"I do not care how soon you betray it, indeed I cannot keep it any longer myself."

"O dear," she thought again, "this is quite hopeless; well, if he *will* bring it upon himself it is not my fault. I have done all I could to keep him from speaking."

"I want your advice," John Featherstonhaugh went on.

"I think I have already given it," Saint replied, looking away toward Maud, and waving her veil in the vain hope that she would come to the rescue.

"But you do not know the circumstances of the case. It's the old story. I want to know whether you think I can make myself worthy of some one of whom I am very fond."

"It isn't a question of being worthy. It is whether she cares sufficiently for you."

"And you are in the position to give me that information. A touch to the rudder now may give a different direction to my life's course.'

Saint was driven to desperation. "I had rather you had not asked me the question," she replied, "for I am sure my answer will not

WINDSOR CASTLE.

please you." It was on her lip to add: "I do not wish to marry *any* one. I could never care for any person as I do for my music,"— but something made her pause, and ask abruptly, "but you have not told me who she is?"

That evening Maud wrote from Windsor: —

"DEAREST BARB, — We are having the most charming time conceivable. I sent you the pencilled jottings in my diary from Marlow,

VIEW OF RICHMOND HILL.

but I neglected to tell you that I have urged Mrs. Isham to make a visit at her father's house while you are there. I believe you only can permanently cheer her up. You are a sunbeam, Barb, and it is your province in life to gladden people's hearts. And you will always have your hands full. You know Confucius says, 'Make happy those that are near, and those that are far will come.'

"We had a very pleasant run down the river from Marlow, with a good deal of towing, while Dick and I had charge of the lines. I should judge that Saint and John Featherstonhaugh had some very interesting conversation. At least they were quite oblivious to the most remarkable points in the scenery, and allowed us to walk along the tow-path until I was nearly ready to drop, without once offering to take the lines. Moreover Saint's attitude toward the young man has entirely changed. 'He seems to meet with your unqualified approval,' I said to her just now, and she replied that she had never had but one objection to him. 'Then he has not freed his mind?' I asked. 'Completely, and I think he was rather pleased with my answer.' I must confess that I was thunderstruck. 'You don't mean to say that you encouraged him!' I exclaimed.

"She smiled in her calmest and most provoking way. 'All in my power,' she said, and refused to add another word. However, she has promised to tell me everything to-morrow when I go out to sketch Windsor Castle.

"Dick has gone back to Oxford, and John Featherstonhaugh has also departed, but he is to show us over the Castle to-morrow. We are staying at the "Star and Garter" of the Merrie Wives of Windsor, for merrie maids are we. Everything hereabouts is very fascinating, but we can only stop long enough for a peep at Stoke Pogis, where Gray wrote his "Elegy;" then Hampton Court, Richmond, and London, with its solid work at South Kensington.

"My light burns low.

"I subjoin Saint's list of Thames River hostleries: The Plough, the Crown and Thistle, King's Arms, the Nag's Head, the Rising Sun, the Anchor, the Swan, White Hart, the Lamb, the Feathers, the Beetle and Wedge, the Leather Bottle, the Bull, the Miller of Mansfield, the Elephant and Castle, Cross Keys, the Dreadnought, the French Horn, the Angel, Red Lion, the Catherine Wheel, Carpenters' Arms, Two Brewers, the Bear, the Flowerpot, George and Dragon, the Anglers, Fisherman's Retreat, Saracen's Head, Star and Garter, the Crown and Cushion, Royal Oak, Royal Stag, Morning Star, Bells of Ousley, the Packhorse, the Cricketers, the Horseshoes, the Old Manor, the Magpie, the Mitre, the Griffin, the Outrigger, the Ram, the King's Head, Three Pigeons, Compasses, Old Ship, and the London Apprentice. Are they not amusing?"

CHAPTER VIII.

BARBARA'S LOG. — CHIP THE FIRST.

JUNE was dying into July. The air, even at the Peak, was warm and close, while at Manchester it was suffocating. Barbara's little charge had entirely recovered, and was running merrily about the house, winning all hearts with her childish prattle; but Barbara herself drooped. She lay listlessly upon the sofa, only rousing to hear Joe's lessons or to aid in stitching the little frocks which Mrs. Atchison had cut for Tina. She was not really ill, she declared, as Mr. Atchison took her languid hand in his large and kindly one, only tired; she would be rested by-and-by.

"I'll tell you what will rest you, and what we all need," he replied, "a yachting trip. It is time we organized our cruise in the " Coal-Scuttle." Dick will be back from Oxford in a few days. Tom can't leave his business at Worcester, poor fellow, but we'll invite Gladys to represent him, and we'll have Ethel up from Great Marlow. Your friend was right when she wrote that only you, Barbara, could cheer her and draw her out of herself, but you can't do that without cheering up a little yourself first. Joe shall go too; we'll put him in as assistant engineer, the butler shall be steward, and one of the housemaids stewardess. Dick shall run down to Liverpool and engage two or three able seamen as crew, and we'll load in a cord or so of novels as ballast. Then we'll pack the baby off to the Asylum, weigh anchor, and you shall keep the log. What do you say to the plan, eh, Barbara?"

"I like it all but the leaving out of Tina. Why not take her with us?"

"I am afraid she will remind Ethel too strongly of the little one she has lost. However, it may not be so; we will see how the child affects her when she arrives."

"Where shall we go, Cousin Acherly?"

"From the Isle of Man to the Isle of Wight. This will take us down the Welsh coast and along the south of England. Then we could have your friends from London to meet us, and make a run with them across the channel. Or, if you are tired by that time of salt-water, we'll send the crew back with the yacht, and we'll go up to London ourselves, and spend a few weeks in town. Ah! your color begins to brighten! That's good. We'll sail at the earliest possible moment."

Barbara in looking over her effects to decide what should fill the lockers of her stateroom, opened once more the silver-hasped desk which had once belonged to her great-aunt Atchison. "Uncle Acherly spoke of laying in a supply of novels," she said to herself. "I am sure these letters look a great deal more fascinating. Why, here is one from Lady Morgan, the authoress, and another from the Countess of Craven, who was once an actress at Covent Garden, and here is quite a little packet from Her Grace the Duchess of Devonshire, the friend of Fox and the Whigs. We will keep them for rainy-day reading in the cabin, for I am sure that Gladys will be as much interested in them as I."

Just then her eye fell upon her unfinished essay. "I'll put that in too," she thought; "perhaps I shall feel bright enough to complete it before the voyage is over. I imagined that I should have read it ere this and fancied I was to achieve a real triumph. Instead of that I've wasted half the summer and accomplished nothing worth speaking of. What a good-for-nothing girl I am!"

Mrs. Isham arrived a few days later. To the surprise of every one Tina seemed to exercise a very happy influence upon her. She insisted on relieving Barbara of her care, and took upon herself the task of finishing the small wardrobe. She even wrote home for certain articles which had belonged to her own little daughter.

"I do not know how this will end," Mrs. Atchison said to Barbara, "If Ethel's interest in the child increases during the voyage she will never consent to part from her."

"Will Mr. Isham be likely to favor her adoption?"

"I cannot say. He will meet us at the Isle of Wight, and certainly this is a very auspicious beginning."

On a sunshiny day in July, when only flying clouds were scudding like white sails across the sky to give countenance to the falling barometer, the high-sided, tight little steam-launch dropped down the Mersey, its muddy tide bringing out the old jest, —

"The quality of mercy is not strained."

AUGUSTUS.

The party on board were full of spirits; they inspected every detail of the little craft, and had lavished their praise on the bright brasses, the neat linen, the shining glass, the mahogany fittings, and the finely-working machinery. They had taken camp-chairs on deck, and Barbara was already beginning her log with statistics relative to course, speed, wind, and barometer. We shall not take literal bits from this log, for these are just the matters for which we do not care, while the occurrences which we would most like to know, the conversations to which we would care to listen, were not written.

Suddenly the coffee-colored water merged into green, and they were on the Irish Sea. It was a chopping sea, and the "Coal-Scuttle" pitched unpleasantly. Moreover, there was now a hint of rain in the atmosphere, and the decks were growing moist and slippery.

"Let us seek the seclusion which the cabin grants," sang Barbara; and the party with one accord went below, Harry clamoring for an early luncheon. But here it presently transpired that Augustus, the dignified footman, who was to act as steward, was very sea-sick, and Bessie, the maid, found it quite impossible to solve the mysteries of the pantry. Mrs. Atchison and Barbara at once set to work, and a satisfactory meal was soon spread. With the exception of Augustus, none of the party suffered from sea-sickness, and after luncheon all donned their mackintoshes and mounted for a short time to the deck. Then followed games of chess and reading about the cozy cabin table, and all were surprised when Mr. Atchison announced that the passage, seventy-five miles, had been made and that the Isle of Man was in sight. The weather had cleared and the sun was setting as they entered Douglas Bay; their first day's voyage was over. They devoted only two days to the island, making the tour in wagonettes, and having the yacht meet them at the Peel, on the Irish Sea. They visited the castle so connected in its associations with "Peveril of the Peak," and Barbara invested in the wooden spoons sold as souvenirs, and the pictorial note-paper on which to write letters to Saint and Maud. The queer device so inappropriately styled the *Arms* of Man — consisting of three human legs, apparently in rapid retreat — met their eye everywhere and never failed to excite their laughter. They commented upon the soft dialect with its use of "wass," so markedly resembling that of the Princess of Thule; they sought out runic stones; and Barbara jotted down a number of fairy stories religiously believed in by an old crone who repeated them to her. One was of an elf-child, left in a human home and nursed and brought up by the mother, who mistook it for her

own, which had been carried away by the fairies. One night the mother missed her charge, and following found it dancing on the birch with its fairy companions. When the elves saw that they were observed they all vanished, and neither changeling nor stolen child was ever seen again.

Gladys and Barbara were continually together, and Mr. Atchison smiled as he saw how kindly was the glance which the undemonstrative English girl often bent upon his niece. Barbara was speaking to her one day of Saint. "You don't like her," she said, impulsively, "but it is because you do not know her. I wish I could say something to make you understand her, for it is very important that you should like each other."

"How important?" Gladys asked, carelessly.

Barbara flushed and hesitated. "Because English people and Americans seem predetermined not to approve of one another."

"I think the reason I do not take greatly to her," Gladys replied, "is because she is very English. We are too much alike for me to care for her, as I do for you, for instance."

From Man, hugging the coast of Anglesey, the "Coal-Scuttle" dropped down to Carnarvon Bay. Dick informed Barbara that he knew this portion of Wales intimately, having done it on foot a few years before with his Brother Tom and John Featherstonhaugh.

"We had on a natural-history mania at the time, I remember," he said. "We found one hundred and fifteen varieties of sea-weed, and counted up one hundred and fifty-four marine animals suitable for aquaria."

"Oh! how could you think of such things!" Barbara exclaimed, for each turn of the boat added a new effect to the superb panorama of town, castle, mountains, and sky. "What glorious mountains! I had no idea there was anything like them this side of the Alps."

"That peak is Snowdon, which we have planned to climb. Aberglaslyn lies away to the right," explained Mr. Atchison.

"I have brought my Alpenstock," said Gladys, "both for use and because I have the vanity to wish another famous name carved upon it."

"What a wild, grand country Wales is,", said Barbara. "I don't wonder that it is the land of Merlin, the enchanter, and the birthplace

BARDIC CONTESTS AT CARNARVON CASTLE.

of so many of the Arthurian legends. It is a country that insists on *largeness* of the imagination."

"That word largeness is rather odd," Dick replied, "but it has a certain fitness all the same."

"Well, now that we are here," suggested Mr. Atchison, cheerily, "what say you to a visit to the castle before dinner? It gives one the same impression of vastness and grandeur."

"What order of architecture does it belong to?" Barbara asked,

CARNARVON CASTLE.

as she looked up admiringly at its massive walls of gray limestone and millstone grit.

"It was built by Edward I., in the thirteenth century," Dick replied, "and I remember that John Featherstonhaugh was interested in making drawings of every part, and quoted Sir Christopher Wren to prove that it was a specimen of the primitive Gothic introduced into Europe at the time of the Crusaders, from the Saracens and Moors."

"To see the castle at its best," remarked Gladys, "we should be here at the time of the 'Bardic Contests,' the national festival. Then, I believe, the court is filled with bazaars, and gay with flags and peasant women in plaid shawls and peaked hats."

"Who is that queer figure over the entrance," Barbara asked.

"That is King Edward," Mr. Atchison replied; "and on the other side of the castle we have the 'Queen's Gate,' named from Queen Eleanor. The castle must have been perfectly impregnable at the time that it was built, and it has nobly stood the assaults of the most formidable of generals, Time. Only the 'Eagle Tower,' the one with the battlemented roof and the slender turrets yonder, has been restored."

They remained over night in their yacht, and early next morning chartered a stage-coach for Snowdon, by way of Llanberis. Mr. Atchison had intended that Joe should remain with the crew in the yacht, but he begged so hard to be taken with them that Barbara interceded in his behalf. "I never seen any real mountings like that, miss," he pleaded, "and besides, it's a mighty wild country, and somethin' might happen to you, miss, if I wasn't along."

The others laughed at the idea of Joe constituting himself Barbara's protector, but they humored his fancy and allowed him a seat on the rumble. The younger members of the party preferred the outside of the vehicle, and as the scenery was increasingly grand, the route running between beautiful lakes, rocky precipices, fantastic peaks, and frightful chasms, the ride was one continual exclamation of surprise and delight. Now, Barbara and Dick had a discussion, as to whether the bird dropping majestically from a pine on a lofty crag were an osprey or an eagle. Now they paused by the side of a deep, still lake for Harry to scramble down and secure some of the exquisite waterlilies; and again they passed some comical peasant women in an absurd steeple-hat, or drew rein at the foot of Castell Dolbadarn, now a picturesque ruin, but in the thirteenth century the most important fortress in North Wales. Barbara and Gladys sat side by side, and more than once in that memorable ride their hands clasped in mute awe before the stupendous masses of rock and the grandeur of the cataracts of the Ceunant Mawr. The region has been appropriately called "a district of disorder, a place where woods, and waves, and winds, and waters were mingled together in the shapeless majesty of chaos."

WELSH PEASANT.

At the village of Llanberis they secured the services of a son of Moses Williams, the celebrated Snowdonian guide, and leaving the coach at the hotel, after a trout supper prepared to climb the mountain by moonlight. The ascent was not difficult, and they paused from time to time to look back at the lakes, stretching like dark mirrors, with the moonlight pouring a silver shimmer over crag and forest. Suddenly a monument of mist came billowing up a defile and wrapped Snowdon all around like a winding-sheet. They crept close to their guide, and Barbara's arm twined more clingingly about Gladys' resolute form. It was neither dark nor light; they appeared to be in a region bewitched; the cloud-forms as they approached were gigantic, towering over the mountain peaks seen through their rifts, but dim and spectral with a cool, soft touch as though they were wraiths of Merlin and his fellow-wizards. And now they were in the fog; wreath after wreath curled and broke about them, only disclosing a more impenetrable gray wall beyond. Their faces were wan and indistinct, and their very voices sounded hollow. All at once the girls discovered that they were alone. The others had passed on more rapidly and had left them behind. They hurried forward and called aloud, but there was no answer.

IN THE MIST.

"I am afraid we have missed the way," Barbara exclaimed, breathlessly, "I do not see any path; is it possible that we are lost?"

"It is no great matter if we are," Gladys replied, reassuringly, "they will send Mr. Williams back after us, and there is not the slightest danger. I think, however, we had better not go on, for we will probably only diverge more and more from the right direction."

They sat down upon the soft heath, and Gladys drew the younger girl close to her, wrapping her tenderly in her own Scotch shawl.

"Come under my plaidie," she said, cheerfully, "and we will have a cozy time all alone together."

"We do seem alone, do we not?" Barbara replied, with a slight shiver; "I never experienced such an overpowering sense of loneliness in my life. Only we two in the whole wide world. Even the world has vanished, it is only we two in space. This must be something like dying, only one is all — all alone then."

"Oh, no," Gladys replied, gravely and sweetly, "there is One who has promised to be with us even then."

They were quiet for a few moments, and then Barbara asked, "Did you not hear a faint, far-away cry as though it were down in some chasm? There are no wolves on Snowdon now, are there?"

"No indeed, and I heard nothing; but I can't help thinking that it would be far pleasanter if John were here."

"It's odd, but I was thinking of your brother too; and, Gladys, now that we are alone, dear, I want to tell you why it is that I am so anxious that you should like Saint."

"I do like her, I am sure I never said that I did not, I only like you better. But what is the famous reason?"

"Only this, that I think she may be your sister some day."

Gladys did not reply, the wall of mist seemed to have drifted in between them, and Barbara went on eagerly: "You do not like it, I know, but you will as you come to know her; she is so very good, and she will come into property — a relative, no a friend, is to give her a comfortable little dowry when she marries."

"I do not think John would care for money considerations," Gladys replied, coldly.

"No, of course not, but they are not to be despised all the same, and I thought you ought to know about it."

"I like her even less for it, little Barbara. Brother John and I have been so dear to one another that I shall have to love his choice very much not to be jealous of her. I do not know where his eyes could have been to prefer Miss Boylston to some one else I could mention."

Barbara started up. "There is that noise again, and hark! O Gladys, *it is* a wolf."

Gladys uttered a shrill, far-reaching "Coo-ee!" an African bush-cry which she had learned from some returned travellers. The sound came back to them not as an echo, but an articulate halloo! and a moment later a bulk came plunging through the fog, apparently unrolling successive envelopes of mist, until Joe stood before them, breathless, but with a glad light on his face. "I told em I'd find you first," he exclaimed. "You be'nt either of you hurt in any way?"

"Not in the slightest," Gladys replied; "unless Barbara has taken cold, for she has had a thorough wetting."

"Cheer up!" Joe remarked, encouragingly; "there is hot coffee at the Summit House, and you are nearly there."

Then he blew a loud blast on a tin horn, with which each member of the search party had provided himself, as a signal that the lost were found, and offering an arm to each he assisted them up to Mr. Philip Williams' refreshment rooms, where a warm welcome awaited them. After warmth and food had done their work of cheer, they stepped out of doors once more to see the sun rise. It was a magnificent spectacle: first a glare of red through the mists unrolling and billowing away from the mountain; then a disc of gold, and the clouds parted, showing the Menai Straits, curving like a silver ribbon. Anglesey purple beyond, and the Isle of Man a distant speck on the sapphire ocean. The lakes below partook of different colors as the light reached them, first black, then deep blue, and finally opalescent as they flashed back the sunrise.

Mrs. Isham repeated softly one of Richardson's verses, —

"The scene is steeped in beauty,
And my soul,
No longer lingering in the shroud of care,
Doth greet creation's smile; the gray clouds roll
E'en from the mountain peaks, and melt in air.'

But Barbara, with her eyes filled with tears, was silent.

They descended the mountain on the other side, resting at a hotel at the foot, and waiting for their stage coach to be brought around with Mrs. Atchison and Tina, who had not attempted the ascent.

PONT ABERGLASLYN.

After a refreshing sleep they drove down the pass of Nant Gwynant, by the Llyn or lake of the same name, and Merlin's Fort, to the Beddgelert, where they passed the night. Here they visited the grave of Gelert and came upon ground which Agassiz had studied and made support his theory of the glaciers. The next day's staging brought them through the famous pass of Aberglaslyn. They passed women in stove-pipe hats, and men, too, knitting as they tended their sheep on the rocky hill-sides; and they strapped their guide-books tight over specimens of " Parsley and delicate Film Ferns."

Their last day of coaching carried them back to Carnarvon and to the " Coal-Scuttle," and they were soon ploughing their way through the blue waters of Cardigan Bay, with Snowdon and its mists as unreal to them as the legends of Merlin.

The next afternoon it happened that as Barbara sat alone on deck under the awning in the stern, Mr. Atchison mounted the companion-way and came to her.

"Where are the others?" he asked, bringing a camp-stool to the side of her reclining chair.

" They have gone forward with Dick. He assured them that they could see the bathers at Aberystwith with his glass; but I did not care to try. I am a little lazy, I am afraid."

Mr. Atchison took her hand kindly. " That experience at Snowdon was a little rough for you," he said.

"Cousin Acherly," Barbara remarked abruptly, "I have never asked you about the legacy which Aunt Atchison left me, but now I would like if you please to understand it."

Mr. Atchison rubbed his forehead thoughtfully. "I don't quite understand it myself," he said. " A part of it is very simple. The legacy itself is Featherstonhaugh Manor " ——

Barbara sat erect. " How did Aunt Atchison come to own that?"

"Gladys' father was a great spendthrift, and he mortgaged it to her for money lent him."

"Then Featherstonhaugh Manor belongs to me!"

"Under certain restrictions, and here comes in the part which is a little vague. The will mentions a codicil, No. 3, and that codicil is not to be found, though it would probably explain everything. The Manor is yours, unless some member of the Featherstonhaugh family puts in a claim for it subject to certain conditions explained in the lost codicil before January next, in which case you will have to be contented with a thousand pounds from the 'contingency and charity fund,' instead."

"And do the Featherstonhaughs know this?"

"John, but not Gladys. He thought it would only worry her, and perhaps she might not be able to keep it from her mother. He hopes to rent the property from the owners, and that all may continue during his mother's life just as it is."

"And has he made no effort to find the lost paper?"

"At first we fancied that it might be among his father's effects. We searched thoroughly but without success, and John has given up all hope of its discovery."

"Of course you looked through that desk you gave me."

"Yes; there is nothing in it but correspondence."

Barbara sighed. "I am sorry matters are in such a twist," she said. "I had hoped it would be simpler."

"Oh! you are nicely provided for in any event."

"Cousin Acherly, I am afraid you'll be displeased with me, — but I have disposed of that legacy."

"Child! What do you mean?"

"I have made out a paper conveying it to Saint."

"But what good can landed property in England do your friend, Miss Boylston?"

"She may decide to settle here. She has no property of her own, and will make a better use of it than I could."

Mr. Atchison's shaggy brows settled down in real displeasure.

"And she accepted the gift, I presume, as simply as if it were a box of gloves."

"She does not know of it as yet. I gave the paper into Maud's keeping to give to her at the proper time."

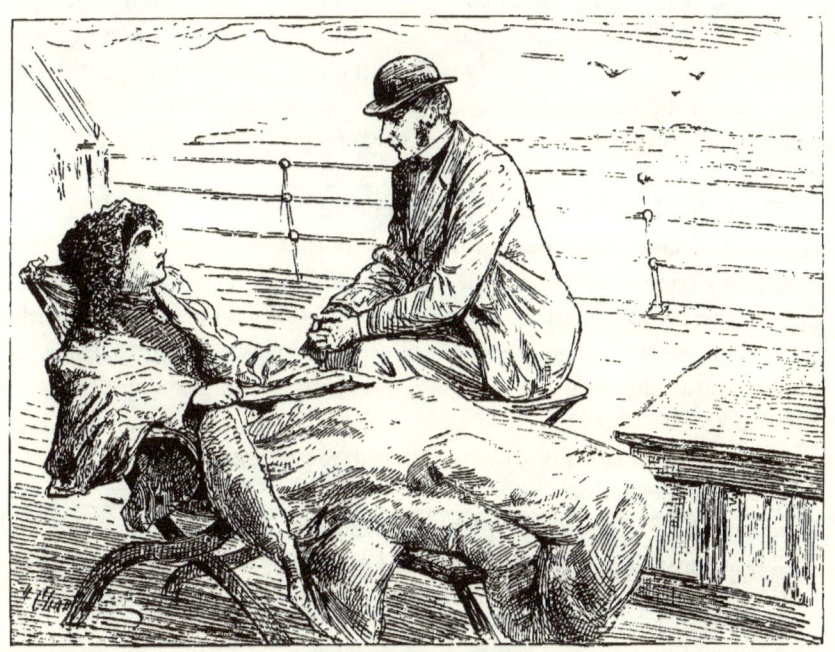

A TALK ABOUT BUSINESS.

"Well, of all absurd, preposterous things! I have heard of schoolgirl friendship, but this surpasses everything. The matter was complicated enough before, but you have got into a hopeless muddle. We shall have to go to chancery to straighten it out. Are you sure that you know how to make out a conveyance that will stand in law."

"It was very simple, but I tried to make it quite clear. I simply wrote: 'I, Barbara Atchison, relinquish all title to property falling to me through the bequest of my great-aunt, Elizabeth Atchison, of

Rowsley, in Derbyshire, England, in favor of Cecilia Boylston, of Boston, Mass.' Then I dated it and signed my name, and Maud witnessed my signature."

Mr. Atchison pressed his lips together firmly. "You have less sense than I thought," he said; "you are an impulsive simpleton."

He turned upon his heel and left her abruptly, and the tears welled up in Barbara's eyes, for she was deeply hurt. Tina ran by just then, and she stretched out her arms to the child, who only shook her pretty curls, and replied, "Me don't want you; me want my Mamma Isham."

Even the baby whom she had nursed back to life had turned against her, and it seemed to Barbara at that moment as if she had lost every friend in the world. The water had turned from blue to green; there was a capful of wind coming freshly up and bearing with it ominous masses of gray cloud. She went below feeling that it was quite natural that the sky should be overcast, and she lay down in her little berth, listening desolately to the gurgling and sobbing of the water along the sides of the yacht, and the whistling of wind in the rigging. When Mrs. Atchison looked in to announce dinner she begged to be excused, saying that she did not feel well.

"Not sea-sick, I hope," replied the good lady. "Well, it is a little rough. I will send you some bouillon, and you must try and make yourself take it."

When Barbara awoke a new day was shining brightly; there had been no storm during the night, and the yacht was rising and falling at anchor. From her port-hole she could make out the towers and chimneys of some city, when dash came a bucketful of water into the room. She had neglected to close the bulls-eye, and the hands were scrubbing down the decks. She could hear animated conversation in the cabin. "We passed 'St. David's Head' in the night," Dick exclaimed. "You know he is to Wales what St. Patrick is to Ireland."

Harry piped up immediately, —

> "There were three jolly Welshmen,
> As I have heard them say;
> And they all went a hunting,
> 'Twas on St. David's Day."

Barbara hastened her dressing and joined the merry party at the breakfast-table. Mr. Atchison greeted her cheerfully; perhaps his heart smote him a little for his harsh words of yesterday.

"Here we are in Milford Haven," he said. "There are interesting places all about, and we must be on shore as much as we can."

They landed opposite Milford on the Pembroke side of the bay, and gave the morning to an inspection of Pembroke Castle. Then, lunching at the "Golden Lion," they took the afternoon train for Carmarthen, one of the most ancient towns in Great Britain. They spent the night here, and rambled about its steep and crooked streets the next morning. Harry insisted that Gladys would need her Alpenstock to aid her in surmounting the cobble-stone pavement, and offered to carve the name of the principal street upon it as one of the most inaccessible peaks on the list. They had a morning glimpse at the Castle of Carreg Cennin on its precipitous cliff, which they did not attempt to climb, and, taking to the railroad again, dined at noon that day at Swansea. Barbara did not care for the place apart from its beautiful bay, but Mr. Atchison was interested in its smelting-furnaces and forges, for Swansea is the metal emporium of Wales. Lead, zinc, tin, copper, nickel, and iron reign supreme here, while the sky is blackened with the smoke of tall chimneys.

Joe was deeply interested, and filled his pockets with specimen ores till Dick declared that if they were to drop him over the rail of the yacht all the life-preservers on board could not hinder his going to the bottom like a shot. But even as he bantered him he made him a present of a silver nugget, for since the adventure at Snowdon all had been touched by Joe's devotion to Barbara, and showed more than usual kindness to the boy. Barbara herself was touched by it and had said to Gladys, " His gratitude is delightful; he follows me about like a spaniel. I really believe that I have found my forte at last, and that it is teaching."

The yacht lay waiting for them in Swansea Bay, and all of the party with the exception of its commercial head and the mechanical Joe were glad to shake the sooty dust of the town from their garments.

They passed Sker, the *locale* of Mr. Blackmore's romance, and dropped anchor that night at Cardiff, paying a visit the next morning to the castle of the Marquis of Bute, and laying in a full supply of the American canned fruits with which the town is plentifully supplied. "I intend to carry this can of Boston baked beans as a precious souvenir to Saint," Barbara remarked, merrily.

Her depression following her conversation with Mr. Atchison had entirely vanished. There was not a morbid nerve in the girl's splendid physique. She had acted according to the dictates of her unselfish, affectionate nature, and a certain glow of satisfaction, which was not egotism, enabled her to bear the disapproval of even this old friend, whose judgment she so highly valued. Perhaps under his discontent she recognized a certain grudging respect which made him do homage to the girl in spite of himself. At any rate, as the yacht glided into the waters of the Usk, and the party prepared for their excursion to Caerleon, Arthur's famous town, Mr. Atchison playfully suggested that each gentleman should fasten his lady's glove or scarf to his helmet in the old knightly fashion, and set the example by twisting a veil of Barbara's about his hat.

"Let me see, a sleeve is the correct thing, is it not?" asked Dick, snatching an unfinished one of Tina's from Mrs. Isham's work-basket. " Here, Gladys, come stitch it as your favor to my polo " — a red sleeve, broidered with pearls, — and he bound her token on his helmet, with a smile, saying, "I never yet have done so much for any maiden living."

Gladys laughed merrily, the whole party joined in the jest, and set out for the legendary town mounted on sturdy Welsh ponies, the grotesque head-gear of the gentlemen exciting much comment among the natives whom they passed.

The principal relic at Caerleon is Arthur's Round Table, an amphitheatre or vast oval depression which may possibly be the remains of a Roman camp.

"How real this makes the idyls," Barbara remarked. "Do you suppose that Arthur really once —

"'Held court at old Caerleon upon Usk'?

The town is real at any rate, and there is the Usk winding down to the sea. I wonder where the tower stood that Guinivere climbed to see Geraint come with fair Enid, when she looked —

"'Up the vale of Usk
By the flat meadow, till she saw them come,
And then descending met them at the gate,
And clothed her for her bridals like the sun,
And all that week was old Caerleon gay.'"

"Really," exclaimed Dick, "this would be a good point from which to set out for America. I can imagine myself repeating with Sir Bedevere, —

"'But now the whole Round Table is dissolved,
And I, the last, go forth companionless,
And the days darken round me, and the years,
Among new men, strange faces, other minds.'"

"Not darken," said Mr. Atchison, "but lighten — those were the dark ages, and all the laureate's glorification of them is rubbish. We can beat them in true heroism nowadays; why, there's enough sentiment and reckless disregard of common sense locked up in our Barbara here to furnish forth a whole volume of idyls."

Barbara stole a shy look at her uncle's face, but although the voice was gruff the glance was kindly. It was evident that though he did not approve of her business qualifications he had nothing against her heart.

The next day the yacht sailed slowly up the Wye, past Chepstow Castle, with its exciting history in connection with the wars of the time of Charles I., for they were bound for Monmouth and Raglan Castle, the background of George MacDonald's fine historical novel "St. George and St. Michael." There was no white marble horse spouting in the courtyard, no Donald or Dorothy; or "chapel with triple lancet windows and picture-gallery, with large oval lights;" only the great towers with the ivy curtaining their windows with its tapestry. But the pictures created by the novelist were so vivid that imagination came to their aid, and they could have said with him: "Ah, here is a stair! True, there are but three steps, a broken one and a fragment. What, said I; see how the phantom steps continue it, winding up to the door of my lady's

RAGLAN CASTLE.

chamber! See its polished floor, black as night, its walls rich with tapestry, the silver sconces, the tall mirrors; the part-opened window, long, low, carved, latticed, and filled with lozenge panes of the softest yellow-green in a multitude of shades." They could have supplied

CHEPSTOW CASTLE.

all this and much more, for the delightful story was first in their minds.

On a quiet Sunday morning they awoke to find themselves lying at anchor in the Avon at Bristol.

"Those who desire can attend service to-day," Mr. Atchison announced. Once more Barbara joined in the impressive words: "The sea is His and He made it," "and the strength of the hills is His

THE AVON AT BRISTOL.

also." Her heart was filled with a sense of God's protection; there was no misgiving now as to her future, though to one of merely worldly mind it would have seemed more dubious than ever. She walked by Gladys' side silent and content.

Suddenly Gladys remarked: "We shall have letters to-morrow; you know we left word to have them forwarded to Bristol. I would not wonder if there should be one from John."

CHAPTER IX.

MAUD'S SKETCHING TOUR. BULLETIN FOUR: — LONDON.

THE next day Dick brought quite a packet of letters back to the yacht. Barbara had a long one from Maud, and retired at once to her pet reclining-chair under the awning to enjoy its contents.

"SOUTH KENSINGTON, JULY 4.

"DEAREST BARB: — It is an utter shame I have not written you before. I have been driven as a leaf before the wind, trying to cram into each day enough of interest to spice an entire week. I have put my work first, however, since we settled here, and have sent home the designs for the prize dinner-set of which I spoke to you. Beside this I have copied two Turner's, and have joined the modelling class. I am delighted with South Kensington, its museum, and its school. It gives me the finest opportunity for study which I have ever had, and I am trying to make hay while the sun shines.

"Still you must not imagine that I have altogether abjured the world with its pomps and vanities. Lady Gubbins gave us a letter of introduction to a friend of hers, Mrs. Arthur Mayhew, who has a residence in Picadilly, which is quite a social centre. She called on us most obligingly, and invited us to one of her 'small and earlys,'' which we afterward ascertained meant a 'crush,' at a fashionably late hour. Mrs. Mayhew is a different type from any I have yet met in England. She is more like an American, — a Washington woman, for instance. She is a complete woman of the world; neither musical, literary, artistic, nor titled; but clever enough to attract all of these classes to her receptions. She is shy of the æsthetic craze, and told me very frankly why. 'If one dresses according to the French modes,' she said, 'one is quite sure of one's authority; but if one attempts to invent a style of one's own, how is one to be quite sure that it is the correct thing? To be sure there are the portraits as guides, but then if one has any conscience all the interior decorations ought to harmonize with the costumes, and one finds one's self in a muddle.' That is just it. The English study and puzzle their brains, and make art a matter of conscience and theory, but they have no swift intuitions, and would no more dare trust their taste than they would their own ideas of right and wrong in religion. Mrs. Mayhew, by the way, is very high church. She reminds me of Du Maurier's Mrs. Ponsonby de Tomkyns in "Punch," and I amused myself at her reception in picking out all the little Tomkyns world with which those inimitable caricatures have made us familiar. There were the same slim, handsome girls with Greek profiles, the same young men, splendidly developed physically, but with no particular conversational abilities, who took your ironical remarks in the most serious manner possible. There was a German musician from Leicester Square, who played divinely, and was patronized by a ponderous duchess, who might have stood for the drawing of Lady Midas. There were old army veterans who walked as if they were on horseback, and one young poet who attitudinized by the mantelpiece and was fed with compliments. There was even an Academician who sat down opposite one of his own pictures, and never withdrew his mournful gaze from it throughout the whole evening, and a quantity of fat middle-aged, middle-class people, technically named 'Philistines,' who seemed to be there for the purpose of filling up the room, and consuming refreshments.

"There were people who looked honestly bored and unhappy, and others who were affectedly enthusiastic or jovial. There were also a few who sat apart and regarded the company with a superior and analytic air as though they were saying to themselves, 'what fools you all are!' We were entertained during the evening by a ballad sung by a representative of the Æsthetic Clique in a 'greenery yallery' gown. Her fingers dabbled with the keys in a limp, nerveless manner that reminded me of an invalid duck paddling feebly in a brook, and there was not wanting a Maudle who posed in pretended ecstacy. Last of all there was a *quantum suff.* of interesting and

THE ÆSTHETIC CLIQUE.

agreeable people as well, among whom I must mention a retired army officer, who has lived a large part of his life in India, and who finds himself almost as much a stranger in London as we are. Everything is changed, he says; the clubs, society, politics, the papers, all belong to a different London from the one he knew. So even slow-going

England progresses, and perhaps she is not so much of a tortoise as we in the vain pride of our youthful, rapid acting, rapid thinking, have imagined. One thing impresses me more and more. When we say England we must not think of this insignificant little island only, but of the vast empire scattered all over the world which owns the good queen's sway. We have prided ourselves on being cosmopolitan just because foreigners from every nation come to us. But England has a better right to the word, for she goes everywhere, plants England where she goes, and brings a little of whatever is admirable home with her. Nearly all the people whom I conversed with at Mrs. Mayhew's had travelled. One otherwise totally uninteresting old merchant had lived in Canton, and had a great deal to tell me of the English colony in China; and there was a very sweet-faced, low-voiced woman who had lived in Cape Town, Africa, until her husband, an astronomer, who had gone out for scientific purposes, died of one of the dreadful fevers. I noticed one young lady who I was sure was an American, — from Kansas City or possibly Denver, there was such a railroad, stocky, gold-miney look about her. She was not in the least vulgar, but bewildered and overpowered by the newness of things. She was very elegantly dressed in the height of the fashion, with rather too many diamonds, but her manner was neither loud nor pushing; she simply sat in a corner and listened, and looked with great hungry eyes. I went up to her and said that I was sure I had found a compatriot; but she was from some new town in Australia, where her father had emigrated when she was a little child, and where he had evidently made a fortune. Mrs. Mayhew brought up her brother, an officer of the Scots Guards, recently returned from Egypt. He was very nice to us both, and chatted away until the poor little Australian princess was quite at her ease. It appeared that she had returned by way of the Suez canal, and had seen the country over which the captain had marched. He explained to us some of the curiosities which we had seen in the Egyptian Court at the Crystal Palace, but had not at all understood. We took our cream on the staircase in real American fashion, and he ran up to his room for a map and explained the attack upon Tel el Kébir in a most interesting way. I thought it very considerate and nice in him.

"Of course we have managed to do some sight-seeing. It would never do to be in London and not visit Westminster Abbey, so we went there first, all very much in the spirit, I must confess, of having it done with, for I fully expected to be disappointed. But Westminster Abbey is one of the things which honorably meet one's expectations. The exterior is gray with age and London grime, but the ivy clings as well as the soot, and the whole effect is very imposing and venerable. It is a flower of the best periods of Gothic architecture, not over-loaded and childishly exuberant, like the later Gothic which we saw in Portugal, but chaste and refined in its richest ornamentation. You must come and see it for yourself, for I despair of giving you any idea of the uplifting sensation given by the combined effect of high, narrow arches, rich stained glass, monumental brass, storied urn, and noble sculptures, intricate wood-carving, and all the blazonry of heraldry and religious symbolism. What struck me most forcibly was not the Poet's corner with its great names, the quiet cloisters, or Henry VIIth's Chapel, the very focus of the whole building, where every art outdoes itself, the wonderful carved ceiling drops its stalactites, the windows burn more intensely, and the armorial banners droop with a proud humility over the canopied stalls, — all this was very sumptuous, but it did not touch my feelings in the least. But the sight 'which angled for mine eyes and caught the water,' as Shakspeare would say, was the tombs of Elizabeth and Mary Stuart. Two chapels, opposite and very similar to each other, are devoted to these queens. Their sculptured effigies lie at full length, Mary's beautiful but passionate face forming an almost living contrast to Elizabeth's haughty features, which could not have been less hard or cold in life. It seemed a little like a petrified sermon on the old text,

WESTMINSTER ABBEY.

'Vanity of vanities,' to see these rivals lying there almost side by side so quietly, all the hatred and heart-burning, the jealousy, intrigue, and relentless cruelty of their lives frozen into silence,—

"'Like burnt-out craters healed with snow!'

"Our first Sunday in London we visited the Foundling Hospital, and some of the little ones there in their quaint caps and aprons, as with folded hands they reverently repeated the Lord's Prayer in the chapel, and later as they partook eagerly of their Sunday dinner, suggested more touching pictures to me than any I have seen in the galleries. That is saying a great deal, too, for I have enjoyed the exhibitions intensely. The National Gallery with its Old Masters, its Turners and Hogarths, and the Royal Academy and the Grosvenor, with their invaluable opportunities for studying the works of the modern English painters. I know you do not care particularly for art gossip, and so I will give you only a homœopathic dose thereof, but I must tell you about the Grosvenor, for there I came across Major Nesbit, the retired army officer from India, whom I met at Mrs. Mayhew's. I spied him across the gallery standing in unhappy meditation before a picture which was not visible from my point of view. He was squinting through his single eye-glass, and steadily sucking away at the head

AT THE FOUNDLING HOSPITAL.

of his cane, as though determined to imbibe inspiration through it.
'What is the matter, Major?' I asked after managing to get quite near

AT THE GROSVENOR.

him. He started and blushed like a young girl. 'I don't understand them at all,' he explained; 'when I was in England before Sir Edwin was all the rage. Sir Edwin understood every beast on the face of the earth, and it really seemed as if they returned the compliment; why, even *I* could understand him, and Sir Edwin understood me.' I laughed as heartily as I dared behind my catalogue. 'Really, Major,' I said, 'I can't allow you to call yourself a beast, though every one at Mrs. Mayhew's seemed inclined to make a lion of you.'

"We were friends at once, and he begged me to take him around the gallery and explain the pictures to him. Strangely enough we admired the same pictures and found that we had much in common. We did not either of us care for Millais, the pet artist of the day, whom he had confused, as so many others do, with the really great French painter Millet. He liked Boughton immensely, and I was proud to be able to claim him and Mark Fisher as Americans, and rather glad that they had submitted to expatriation, if only for the sake of placing worthy American work by the side of the best that England can offer. Alma Tadema's revivals of the classical period interested me more than they did the Major. I believe he even found something to criticise in the architecture, and I could see that he gained in self-respect visibly afterward, and gave his opinions in regard to Herkomer, E. Burne Jones, Hall, Whistler, Walter Crane, and others, with less of the apologetic and the interrogation mark. There was a very creditable portrait by H. R. H. the Princess Louise, and I think the Major thought me very obliging for setting my Americanism aside and frankly liking it. In return he admitted that a portrait by an American girl, Miss Starr, was simply exquisite, and that Leighton's work seemed to him more poetic than realistic, even after he knew that he was president of the Royal Academy. He was loud in the praise of a group of wounded soldiers in a picture which he had seen somewhere else, by Mrs. Virginia Thompson Butler, which he said was drawn with all a woman's sympathy and delicate insight. They have many reminiscences of Mrs. Butler at South Kensington. She studied here before she went abroad, and all praise her earnestness and determination. After all, the English have all our essentially good qualities. If they lack our nerve and go,

DOING LONDON IN HANSOM STYLE.

they make up for it, the best of them, in staying power, and in resolutely, unflinchingly setting their face to do the right so far as God grants them to see the right, which I reverence most devoutly.

"The pictures which I care most for in London are not those of the exhibitions, but the myriad aspects we see of men and manners about us. The panorama of street life, as we see it from the omnibuses, or as we go dashing about doing London in hansom style, — that is, tucked from the driving rain in a buggy-like vehicle, with a rubber robe buttoned across the front of our carriage to the height of our eyes, and our driver perched at a dizzy height behind and above us. The people that we see through the fog remind us strikingly of Dickens. The costermongers, the policemen in their stiff helmets, the wretched poor, the cockney snob, the charity boys in odd costumes, the Sairey Gamps, and the Mr. Dombeys all jostle solemnly, and the absurdity of it all is that they never confess by so much as a nod or a wink that they are only assumed characters in a grand Dickens carnival. And then there were the gamins around about High Holborn and St. Giles, who seemed to have walked out of Hood's poems.

CHARITY BOY.

"Saint will write you of her occupations. She is taking music lessons and reading German preparatory for Munich. We attend the concerts together in the evening. We heard Henschel at one of the Popular Classical Concerts at St. James's Hall last Saturday, and Mrs. Mayhew and her brother took us to one of the Sacred Harmonics at Exeter Hall. The royal family were present, and I had an excellent opportunity to make a sketch of the Princess Beatrice.

"Just now Saint is deeply interested in a course of piano recitals; nothing will tear her from London until they are concluded. But after they are over she has promised to make a sketching tour with me down into the heart of Surrey and Kent. London will be insufferably warm in August, and I mean to get away from it as early as the middle of July. Can't we manage to meet in Guilford? It is not very far from Portsmouth, where you say your cruise will end.

"I put off visiting the Tower for quite a while, for I fancied that I should not enjoy it. I remembered that grand letter which Sir Walter Raleigh wrote his wife from the Tower the night before his execution. I remembered Delacroix's touching picture of the little princes awaiting the coming of their murderers, and I had no heart for trying the edge of the great axe which has kissed so many fair and noble throats. I could have quoted the words which Shakspeare puts into Prince Edward's mouth, —

"'I do not like the Tower of any place.'

"I went because I knew that I would be ashamed to say that I had not seen it, and I was thoroughly glad that I had conquered my aversion. The Tower is not a state prison, alone filled with gloomy memories. It is a huge fortress composed of a mass of different buildings of different periods and varied styles of architecture, and has been used as a royal residence, as treasure-house, and museum, as well as a stronghold, military barracks and dungeon.

"Under William the Conqueror it was made the castle of the Norman kings, and has been added to by nearly every monarch since his time. It is the building of all others which contains within its walls, more vividly than it could be printed within covers, the entire history of England. Even Westminster Abbey is inferior to it in this regard. The bones of the monarchs lie there, it is true, and we have long and

GAMIN.

GAMIN.

lying eulogies to their virtues, but at the Tower are preserved their very acts and lives. In the Horse Armory we have a small regiment of grotesque mounted effigies, each in the identical armor worn by the dead-and-gone monarchs from Edward I., in 1272, to James II., in 1688. Queen Elizabeth's Armory, with its spoil of the Spanish

THE TOWER OF LONDON.

Armada, was another interesting gallery, and the Jewel Tower, with the crown finery, an orderly Aladdin's cave of diamonds, rubies, and sapphires. Some of the most notable buildings included in the tower enclosure are the Middle Tower; the Bell Tower; St. Thomas's Tower with its Traitor's Gate; the Bloody Tower, named from the murder of the children of Edward IV.; the Record Tower; the White Tower; St. John's Chapel; Beauchamp Tower; and the Church of St. Peter.

"I expect to visit the Houses of Parliament next week and to attend service at St. Paul's on Sunday. If I were at the beginning instead of at the end of my letter, I would tell you how I enjoyed the Temple Church, with the effigies of the Templars in chain armor, their legs crossed in token that they had fought in the Crusade, and their shields and swords beside them. The stained glass here is very beautiful, and I do not wonder that Hawthorne, who did not care for pictures at all, thought it the most 'magnificent method of adornment' that human art has invented. The remaining sights of London will doubtless come all in good time.

"It strikes me at this late date that I have told you nothing of our visit to Windsor and to Hampton Court. Well, this letter is already too long, and you will excuse the omission. I told John Feathertonhaugh, before he left us, that you had made over all your property in England to Saint. He seemed intensely interested, and said that he had never heard of such an instance of disinterestedness, and was altogether very appreciative and complimentary.

"How do you enjoy his sister? Saint and Miss Featherstonhaugh were not chemical affinities, and had no appreciable effect upon each other. They were both alkalis, but you are a good deal of an acid, and I should think that bottling you up together in that little test-tube of a yacht might occasion some lively effervescence.

"Saint joins me in love to Mrs. Isham and Mrs. Atchison, and in kindest regards to all the others.

        "Lovingly,   Maud."

Barbara refolded the letter with a little sigh. "Maud is not quite satisfactory, after all," she thought; "she forgets that she has not told me the result of Saint's last interview with John Featherstonhaugh. I would like to know just how it all came about, but Saint will tell me when we meet in Surrey."

Then she opened the letter and read once more. "He was very appreciative and complimentary." Barbara was not pleased with this. She had not intended Maud should tell John Featherstonhaugh of her disposition of her property, and he had evinced too much satisfaction in the arrangement to quite please her. It was natural, perhaps, for most men to be gratified by the prospect of marrying money, but Barbara had imagined that this particular man would be actuated by nobler considerations, and would display on occasion a fine scorn of money matters. She was disappointed in her hero, and she was angry with herself for having made a hero of him. "What does it matter to me?" she said to herself, sternly; "I made the sacrifice not for his sake, but for Saint's;" and then a startlingly audacious voice within her seemed to ask, "Are you quite sure of that?" and before Barbara realized what she was doing, she had torn Maud's unoffending letter across and across, and had tossed the handful of tiny bits over the side of the yacht. They scattered upon the light breeze and settled down to the sea like a flock of white butterflies.

Gladys looked up wonderingly, and Barbara met the unspoken question with a blush. She could not have told why she had so treated her friend's letter.

CHAPTER X.

BARBARA'S LOG. — CHIP THE SECOND.

THE "Coal-Scuttle" was ploughing its way merrily down the Bristol Channel, the sun glancing brightly on the crests of the rather rough water — for the northern and western coast of Devon is wild and rocky, and the channel strewn with sunken crags over which the white caps boil and spout boisterously, even in fine weather.

"You had a letter from home, did you not?" Barbara asked of Gladys.

"Yes, and one from John, too. It seems that he is much disappointed by our tour, for he had planned to spend a week with us at the Peak, his first vacation in many months."

"And now he will not go?"

"He will put it off until we return."

Dick approached them, steadying himself against the wind and keeping fast hold of his cap. "You can't think what that boy Joe is up to," he remarked.

"Has he taken the engineer's place altogether?" Barbara asked.

"No, he has been puttering with the bits of ores he found at Swansea, and has made a very pretty keepsake for you, Cousin Barbara. Here he comes now with his present."

Joe approached respectfully, and handed Barbara a small box, which was found to contain a tiny silver padlock, ingeniously made, and brightly burnished. Barbara overwhelmed the gratified boy with her praise and thanks, and fastened the pretty ornament as a bangle on one of her bracelets.

"It is a sign that my hand and heart are safely locked," she said, merrily.

"The lock will open," Joe replied, practically, without any apprehension of a second meaning in his words, "if a person happens to have the right key."

The others laughed, and Joe went below, filled with supreme contempt at mirth for which he could see no reason.

They were skirting now the northern shores of Somerset and Devon, and the coast became increasingly wild and picturesque. The sea had hollowed out caves in the almost perpendicular face of the cliffs, and the tide ran into them with a low, sullen boom like the report of cannon. Villages clung picturesquely to the sides of the precipices, and lighthouses crowned promontories and gave warning of danger. At Lynmouth the yacht anchored, and the party, mounting on rugged little ponies, set out for an excursion to the Valley of Rocks, the background of the charming romance of "Lorna Doone." The moorland was sweet with the fox-glove, golden gorse, pimpernel, heather, and a hundred other wild-flowers. They found Oare Church, and dined at a farm-house on the eggs and bacon, brown-bread and snowy cream cheese of which John Ridd was so fond. The bog lands lay before them, a rich black in spots, and bright here and there with vivid green patches. The noisy Bagworthy brawled over its rocky bed, and on beyond were the hills which formed the rampart of Glen Doone. They reached the glen at length, and found it full of shapeless masses of rock — an abandoned quarry it might have been, were there any city near to account for it? They tried hard to fancy that these stones might once have formed the regularly-built cottages of the Doones, but they were too irregular in size and shape to pass for ruins; they were plainly the fantastic sport of Nature.

The next day, a fine sunshiny one, was spent on board the yacht. They sat on deck scanning the coast through their opera-glasses.

"I am positive that village clinging to the cliff yonder is Westward Ho!" Dick exclaimed, suddenly.

"Is that the name of a village?" Barbara asked. "I have never read 'Amyas Leigh,' and I always thought 'Westward Ho!' an exclamation or encouraging word of Charles Kingsley's, something like our Horace Greeley's, 'Go West, Young Man!'"

"Ho is a contraction for hold or hight," Mr. Atchison explained. "All of this coast and that of Cornwall, which we are approaching, were dear to Kingsley. It would make a very interesting excursion

COAST BETWEEN TINTAGEL AND BOSCASTLE.

to track his wanderings through this peninsula, but we have not time for it this trip."

They were passing precipitous headlands which plunged abruptly into the sea and threw out a picket-guard of pointed rocks which had evidently once formed a portion of the mainland. "That is Tintagel," Mr. Atchison explained, pointing to a low ruin partly on the mainland and partly on some semi-insulated rocks. "We might run in to see it if we were not anxious to reach Land's End before dark. It is the reputed birthplace of King Arthur."

"I can see it quite well from this point, uncle, and really we have had almost enough of King Arthur, it seems to me."

"Are you tired of him?" Gladys asked. "I think it very interesting to find these places coming up again and again; it is like reading the recurrent numbers of a serial story. We had Merlin in North Wales, the Table Round and Guinivere at Usk, and here we have the coming of Arthur, one of the later legends, you remember."

"I don't remember in the least," Barbara replied, "but we have the poems in book-case in the cabin, and I will run down and get them."

Dick pushed her firmly but gently into her seat, while Harry tumbled gallantly down the companion-way after the volume. The entire family were very kind to Barbara, and would hardly allow her to take a step for herself.

"Take a good look at the castle before we pass it," Mr. Atchison counselled, handing Barbara a powerful spy-glass, and steadying it for her; "we will have time enough for the legend afterward."

"It appears to be roofless and dismantled," Barbara reported, "though I can see some dark slits of windows looking vacantly out toward the sea."

"That bastion on the shore side," Dick announced, "contains a portal called the 'Iron Gate.' It looks oldish enough. I wonder whether it really had anything to do with Arthur, if indeed there ever was such a personage."

"The castle is undoubtedly the work of the early Britons," Mr. Atchison replied. "It is built roughly of slate, joined with coarse mortar, without any attempt at architectural ornament. It was old at the time of the Conquest, and is mentioned in the 'Doomsday Book.'

BOTALLACK MINE.

As to the genuineness of Arthurian legends, I refer you to Gladys here."

" It is true," Gladys said, " that the legends existed before the time of Tennyson. He only collected and beautified them with his genius. And Tintagel has always been popularly considered the birthplace of Arthur. Do you find the name mentioned in the poems?"

Barbara looked up from the book. " Bedivere, in telling the story of the coming of Arthur, says, —

> "'Ye know that in King Uther's time,
> The prince and warrior Gorlois, he that held
> Tintagel, castle by the Cornish sea,
> Was wedded with a winsome wife Ygerne,
> That Gorlois and King Uther went to war,
> And overthrown was Gorlois and slain.
> Then Uther in his wrath and heat besieged
> Ygerne within Tintagel.'

" Here it seems the conqueror king married the unwilling Ygerne, and here Arthur, a child of mists and tempests, was born and passed his childhood. I believe the legends are in great part true; too many noble deeds and words have clustered about Arthur for the character to have been wholly a myth."

" It was a wild place indeed in which to rear an imaginative child," said kindly Mrs. Atchison; " brought up in such weird surroundings, even with no wizard Merlin for a tutor, he might well have fancied strange voices calling him to a mission and fate beyond that of ordinary men. The Cornish miners in those savage-looking clefts are as superstitious as the people of that remote age."

" That is the Botallack Mine, which we are passing now; and the next point of interest," Dick explained, " is Land's End, while twenty-seven miles away are the Scilly Islands, which have wrecked so many home-bound ships. The region between, tradition says, was once solid ground, and was called Lyonesse."

"And there," said Gladys, "we can write *finis* against the Arthurian legends, for it was in Lyonesse, —

"'A land of old upheaven from the abyss,
By fire to sink into the abyss again,'

that Arthur passed from human sight after his last battle with the heathen."

"Spenser calls the spot fairy ground," said Mrs. Atchison, "and

CAPE CORNWALL.

we may expect the small people to play some trick upon us as we sail over it."

"I am more interested in the actual," said Dick. "Just between Land's End and Cape Cornwall is Whitesand Bay; we will anchor there, and go on shore for luncheon at 'The First and Last.'"

"Pray what manner of a place is that?" Barbara asked.

"It is an inn," replied Dick, "which boasts on the landward side of its sign of being the *Last*, and facing the sea asserts that it is the *First* building in England."

They walked along the shore to the hostelry, watching the ships pass on the wide Atlantic. One steamer came up wearily, trailing a long scarf of smoke behind her.

"She has had rough weather," Mr. Atchison said. "One can tell by the freshly piled sea-weed on the rocks that there has been a storm off to the southward; it is well she was no nearer shore when it struck her."

"I wonder if she is from America," Barbara asked.

"The American steamers come in nearer the Irish coast," Dick replied, "more likely she's from the continent. Those are ugly tooth-like rocks off shore, and they have odd names, though it would puzzle a more imaginative mind than mine to tell the 'Shark's Fin' from 'Dr. Johnson's Head.'"

LAND'S END.

They dined royally at "The First and Last" on fresh mackerel broiled to a turn, and a brace of wild duck, which mine host had himself shot. He was very friendly, but seemed anxious to get rid of them.

"The pilchards have been coming in by millions," he said, "a sure sign there's a squall brewing. You'd be getting round the point into safe harbor at Penzance."

The night came down overcast and ominous before they were fairly under way. The wind blew with a long shrill whistle through the rigging, and some sea-mews shrieked by them, as they put the yacht's head resolutely against the wind.

Barbara pulled the hood of her waterproof over her head and held it together with her teeth, while she clung to Mr. Atchison, as he made the rounds of the yacht to see that all was in ship-shape for the night. The others were snugly ensconced in the cabin, but she wished to see more of the fairy regions over the sunken plain of Lyonesse. There was not a star visible, and none of the brilliant phosphorescence which is often seen upon these waters — all was gloom impenetrable.

Suddenly out of the wall of darkness ahead loomed a blacker bulk, and from the bulk glowered a sullen red eye. The little yacht quivered from stem to stern, and then answering to Joe's quick signal, veered suddenly to the left and shot away upon the plunging waters.

"What was it?" Barbara asked, breathlessly, half fancying that some genii had risen from the enchanted waters.

"It was the port light of a steamer," Mr. Atchison replied, "which would surely have run us down if Joe had not been faithful at his watch. Do not tell the others, it would only make them nervous, but we have just escaped a supreme danger. You are very calm; I fancy you do not realize that we have been near eternity."

"We are always near it, are we not?" Barbara replied, quietly. "But He will not take us, we may be sure, while He has anything still for us to do."

"What more do you intend to do, child? It seems to me that you have as good as made your will and withdrawn yourself from this world's concerns."

"Oh! one can serve Him without money, I am sure," she replied, impetuously, "or else He would not have made so many people poor. I have found out that I can teach, and I am going to look for a situation in some charity school, where I can support myself and do good at the same time."

"Nonsense," replied the other, but the words had a more kindly accent than the reproof with which he had first met her disposal of her property.

They went below and found that the others had retired, with the exception of Dick, who intended to take a turn at the watch. Barbara entered her little state-room. The swinging lamp was burning steadily, but everything else seemed at an angle, and she was obliged to support herself against the side of her berth, for the yacht was pitching heavily. She had hardly taken off her hat and wraps, when it lurched still more alarmingly, and in the opposite direction; the ewer fell to the floor with a crash, drenching the rug, and some heavy object was projected from the upper berth to her feet. Her first impression was that the "Coal-Scuttle" had struck a rock, or collided with some other vessel; but as the yacht presently righted herself, and proceeded on her way with perceptibly less pitching than before, she came to the conclusion that it had simply changed its course abruptly, and, Lands' End being completely rounded, was now headed directly for Penzance.

CODICIL. NO. 3.

The projectile which had whizzed so unpleasantly near her ears in its fall proved to be her great-aunt's writing-desk. It now lay upon the floor a total wreck. "I wonder if Joe can mend it," she thought, as she bundled the letters into some empty pockets in her shoe-bag, and pinned them securely in place. "The water-nixies did their worst by us just as we were clearing the enchanted water." She spread the broken pieces of the desk before her on the berth, and as she did so noticed a package projecting from a compartment between the lining and the outer portion. She took it out carefully, but the package had been broken open by the fall; a narrow folded paper lay before her, marked in her aunt's cramped script, "Codicil No. 3." Here it was found at last, either through the spite or favor of the water-nixies. She lay down in her berth, for the movement of the yacht rendered it impossible for her to stand quietly, and read the strange document eagerly : —

"*Whereas, the male representatives of the house of Featherstonhaugh, in Derbyshire, have, so far as I have been able to ascertain, invariably and without exception married for money, and have made all speed thereafter to waste and consume their wives' portions;*

"*And whereas, the present John Featherstonhaugh, of Featherstonhaugh Manor, prepossesses me as an honorable youth and a marked contrast to the men of his race;*

"*Therefore, it is my will that, if this paper shall be discovered before the time appointed in my testament, and the said John Featherstonhaugh be at that time wedded or betrothed to a worthy but portionless bride, or one whom he deems portionless, and that manifestly for no greed of sordid expectations, and with no knowledge of this proviso;*

"*Then my heirs in America shall relinquish all claim to Featherstonhaugh Manor, and my executor shall confirm the same to the said John Featherstonhaugh.*"

The codicil was dated, signed, and sealed. "Why had Aunt Elizabeth hidden it away and left its discovery to an unlikely chance?" Barbara wondered. "Perhaps, because after she had made the provision she half-repented it."

Then the thought came that she need not have conveyed her legacy to Saint, since John Featherstonhaugh would now possess his own under the will. She glanced over the codicil again, "a portionless bride," but Saint was not portionless now, and John Featherstonhaugh knew it. She remembered the unpleasant sensation she had experienced when Maud wrote her of his ill-concealed pleasure following the announcement of her gift to Saint.

There was something else in the packet which had contained the codicil — a gold-mounted miniature. Barbara started, for at first glance it seemed to her that it was John Featherstonhaugh himself. A second look told her that the fashion of dressing was antiquated, and the face, while strikingly like in some features, was also markedly different in expression from that of her friend. It must be the face of his father, and she then fell to studying the differences in the two faces as well as the flickering lamplight would allow, hoping to find in them the key to a difference in character. All the lineaments of John Featherstonhaugh's face stood plainly out from memory.

His father's chin was weaker, the brow more retreating; the mouth was handsome, perhaps, but Barbara did not like the smile, and was sorry that all the other features were so similar. Could it be possible that father and son were both fortune-hunters, and that she had only defeated her aunt's wise purposes by her gift to Saint? She put the paper away, troubled and shaken in mind; she was not sure now that she had acted for the best; but faith lay firmly under all; she had meant it for the best at least, and she was sure that every act performed from right motives would be wisely overruled in the end.

CHAPTER XI.

THE RIGHT KEY.

WHEN she awoke the next morning, the yacht was lying quietly beside the quays of Penzance, the Holy Headland of ancient times.

In the merry bustle which ensued, consequent upon their visiting the handsome city, with interesting fish-market and picturesque fish-

LIZARD POINT.

wives, Barbara had no opportunity to communicate with Mr. Atchison. It was not until afternoon, when they were picking their way at low tide across the long causeway which connects St. Michael's Mount

RYNANCE COVE.

with the mainland, and which lies under water eight hours out of twelve, that she told her uncle of the finding and the contents of the codicil.

"This does not help you at all, that I can see," he replied. "If John can claim the Manor under this codicil,—and I must confer with Gladys to ascertain what probability there is of this,—then the money which was to have come to you as an alternative will go to your friend, Miss Boylston. It really goes against my grain to think of your having cut yourself out in the way you did. However, that is too late for mending, and I have been thinking of your desire to teach or devote yourself to some charitable work. Your aunt left a large sum to be applied to philanthropical purposes. Her idea was that a

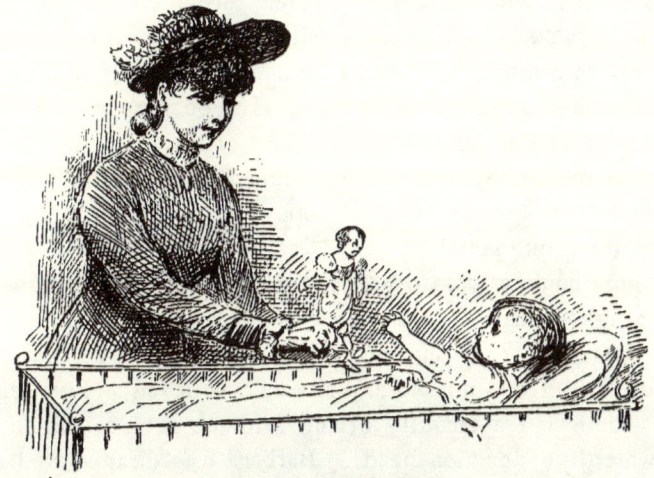

DOLLS FOR THE TINAS.

piece of property should be purchased near Manchester, to be used as a temporary home for the children of factory operatives, with school and hospital attached.

"Her idea was that it should be a little family, that the number of inmates should never exceed ten; that by rotating the guests judiciously a large number might be benefited during the year. There is abundance of money for assistants and all necessary appliances. How would you like the position of Mother Superior?"

"It would be delightful," Barbara exclaimed. "I ask nothing better in life. And could father come out to me when he retires from the army and spend his old age in this lovely English country?"

"Certainly, my child."

"And we will have a workshop for mechanical geniuses like Joe, and a garden for consumptives like Jim, and a kindergarten and dolls for the Tinas, and just the special instruction which each child needs. Oh, Cousin Acherly, I am so impatient to begin."

"It seems to me you have begun already," Mr. Atchison replied, pointing to Joe, who was carrying Tina carefully on his back across the slippery rocks. "I will see about the selection of a proper building on my return to the Peak. I do not so much regret Dick's resolution to emigrate to America now. If you remain in England I shall think that our country has the best of the bargain. You seem to me like one of my own children, and I am glad that you will be near when I am growing old. I hope that America will shape Dick into something like you."

The next landing was at the "Lizard," a rocky point crowned by a double light-house. "It is one of the greatest geologic curiosities on the coast," Dick announced. "The formation is serpentine, of a beautiful dark green, mottled and streaked with red and white."

They collected a quantity of the brilliant pebbles which shone under water like Venetian beads. Barbara was disappointed to find that they lost a part of their beauty when dry, and suggested keeping them in a decanter of water.

"A better idea," Dick thought, "would be to pave the floor of an aquarium with them," and a quantity were laid aside for that purpose.

The little shops with their vases, paper-weights, and bracelets cut from this rock with which the natives tempt souvenir-seeking tourists reminded Barbara of those at Niagara.

The next day they ran in to Plymouth, so connected in every American mind with the setting forth of the Pilgrims. They found it a handsome and thriving town, but possessing little of interest to them apart from its associations. Fourteen miles out at sea stood the famous Eddystone Lighthouse, and they all listened with interest to the story of its noble builder, Smeaton, who fought public opinion and the elements until his dream was a reality. They built by day and at night rowed back to Plymouth, not certain that the morning would show their work still standing. "Again and again the engi-

PLYMOUTH.

neer, in the dim gray of the morning, would peer through his telescope at his deep-sea lamp-post. Sometimes he had to wait long until he could see a tall white pillar of spray shoot up into the air. Thank God, it was still safe!"

From this point they took a long course to the Isle of Wight, for Mrs. Isham was anxious to join her husband, who she knew must be waiting for her by this time at Ryde.

The Isle of Wight was in after years to Barbara a delightful but confused memory of wide-spreading downs, covered with flocks of sheep; of churches that seemed to Barbara the original of certain old drawing patterns with which she had begun a short-lived study of art in her early youth; of exhilarating horseback rides along the under cliff; of cottages with thatched roofs, in one of which lived and died the "Dairyman's Daughter" of Leigh Richmond's touching story, and in another Little Jane; of Osborne House, the summer residence of Queen Victoria, and Shanklin and Black-Gang Chines, wild chasms threaded by wild cascades and adventurous goats. They made their first landing on the island at Ventnor, the "English Madeira," stopping at the successor to the famous Crab and Lobster Inn; and sending the yacht home from this point, for Maud had written that much as she would enjoy it she could not spare time from her work for a cruise. Henceforward their journeying was to be by land, and Barbara, though she delighted in the sea, was glad to strike once more into flowery lanes and fields.

It was at Carisbrook Castle, in the centre of the island, that Mr. Atchison next spoke to Barbara of John Featherstonhaugh. It happened that only they two cared to climb to the top of the Keep for the enchanting view, and while Barbara was resting, her uncle, who had been talking just before of Charles the First's imprisonment here, changed the subject suddenly and remarked, "I have been talking with Gladys, and she thinks that John will claim the Manor under the codicil. She says that she has heard from him recently, and that he is deeply interested in a young woman who will bring him no dowry apart from her own worth."

Barbara looked up quickly. Had John Featherstonhaugh said that when he knew of her gift to Saint? And would he claim the legacy by perjury? It was a great blow; she could not believe he would be so base.

"Gladys said," Mr. Atchison continued, "that she did not think

CARISBROOK CASTLE.

her brother had declared his mind as yet, and agreed to say nothing to him of your discovery until he shall have announced the result of his wooing."

Barbara was so indignant that she hardly took in the meaning of this remark. It seemed to her that John Featherstonhaugh must already know the contents of the codicil, and be shaping his conduct accordingly. "Saint would lose all respect for him if she knew," was her thought. "Shall I tell her? How would such interference look? As if I was envious "——

Barbara rejected the idea hotly, and springing up, turned so suddenly to descend that she stumbled on the first step, and without Mr. Atchison's assistance would have been seriously hurt.

Maud had written that she and Saint would join them at Guilford, in Surrey, Birket Foster's sketching-ground, and through this sweet blossoming country they now drove in a roomy wagonette, which Dick dubbed "the Ark." The trimly-clipped hedges and prim garden-walks seemed just the spots for Kate Greenaway figures in mob-caps and long mits to take tea in painted cups, with bread and butter and marmalade.

They passed pools willow-shaded and quiet,

"Where the long green reed-beds sway,
In the rippled waters gray."

and hedges pink with wild roses and yellow with broom. The orchards had lost their blossoms, but were crisp with freshly washed, intensely green leaves, and the wind rippled the eye with just the dimples which it gives to quiet water.

Barbara sang softly,—

"Summer is a-coming in—
Loudly sing, cuckoo!
Groweth seed and bloweth mead,
And springeth wood anew."

They came across a gypsy camp in a knoll, and stopped to buy some of the sweet-grass baskets which an old woman was braiding. The crone offered to tell Barbara's fortune, and the others insisted upon hearing it. She took the girl's fair palm in her own and scanned its lines carefully. The little padlock-bangle at the wrist caught her eye, and she said at once. "The young miss's heart is locked fast, let us see what kind of key will open it." Then she bent the pink finger-tips downward, muttering as she looked at the little finger and the others in succession.

"Not a golden key, that is too small to fit the lock; not love alone, that is too weak to move the strong bolts. It will be a title maybe. No! My lord may carry that key to another door. Mayhap it is cleverness, and the lass is ambitious-like, and the key that shines bravest that will slip the smoothest. Eh! but the lass is fearsome hard to please. Come, the forefinger is near as long as the middle; it's honor then that leads; it's the key that's straight and not crooked, and the lad that knows his right hand from his left, and is never left-handed—that will win."

"You've hit it, dame," Mr. Atchison exclaimed, giving the old woman a crown.

"I don't know about that," Harry objected. "Cousin Barbara isn't a bit gloomy and religious; she's the jolliest girl I ever met."

"Can't one be jolly and a stickler for principle, too?" Gladys asked, but Harry shook his head doubtfully.

"We shall have to put down the sides of the carriage," Dick remarked, as they took their places. "We will have a race with a shower."

After all, the shower overtook them before they reached Guilford, and came down with a will, blurring out the landscape and filling the road with tawny pools, through which they splashed merrily. They entered Guilford by a beautiful ridge, with an atrocious name, the "Hog's Back." A rainbow spanned the town with a superb double arch; and Saint was looking out of an upper window as they dashed up to the inn door.

How the girls chattered when they were fairly together. Jest and story, and snatches of song, and peals of laughter, bounded back and forward like balls in a tennis-match. It was not until they were alone together, however, that confidences were exchanged. Maud had discovered a picturesque stable near a thatched farm-house, and the girls set out for a day in the fields in this pleasant garden-land of England.

Maud had received bad news from home. Her father had met with reverses which compelled him to live in a much narrower way. "When the funds which I have now on hand are exhausted," she explained, "I shall have to go home and in some way support myself. I have laid aside enough for my return passage, and find that I can remain two months longer. I thought that I might put in a week's sketching profitably here in the country, and then I shall go back to London and lay up corn for the seven years of famine."

Maud was as self-reliant, as cheerful and businesslike as ever. The emergency had weighed her in the balances, and she had not been found wanting.

"But what will you do?" Barbara asked.

"Teach," Maud replied, "if the worst comes to the worst, but I hate teaching, and I hope to find china-decorating enough to keep me in salt."

She could not have been more composed if she had known the truth that the situation which she desired was already hers, and at that very moment the committee had awarded the first premium to her designs for a dinner-set, and a noted manufacturer was penning a letter inviting her to the superintendence of his designing department.

"I am glad that Maud will stay into the fall," Saint remarked, "for in October I mean to go on to Germany."

"And how about John Featherstonhaugh?" Barbara asked.

Saint smiled queerly.

"Shall we tell her now?" she asked. "You may," Maud replied, 'I feel as if I had been so thoroughly taken in by the whole matter that I haven't the face to say a word." And so saying she closed her

color-box with a snap, and shouldering her sketching umbrella tripped briskly toward the farm-house on a pretended quest for stale bread for artistic purposes.

"Barb, dear," Saint began, twisting a daisy-stem about her third finger in an embarrassed way, which seemed to Barbara very pretty and becoming, when one considered the circumstances. "Barb, dear, I am afraid you are not at all prepared for what I have to tell you."

"Maud has done a good deal to enlighten me," Barbara replied, "and then I've not quite lost the use of my own eyes, you know."

"Please don't be frivolous; it is a very serious matter, at least to John Featherstonhaugh, and I am almost as much interested as he."

"Naturally," Barbara remarked, dryly.

"O dear! why will you persist in misunderstanding; well, I must explain as fast as I can. You know he said in Portugal that I reminded him of his sister, and that he had great confidence in my opinion and all that, and so, I don't know exactly how it came about, but while we were floating down the Thames we were very confidential."

"Naturally," Barbara commented again.

"Don't speak in that way, Barb, you put me all out."

"Well, dear, I won't tease you any more. He was very confidential, and he told you that he was deeply in love with a certain young person, and desired that person's views on the subject, wasn't that it?"

"Exactly. No, I could not give him the young person's views, and he did not imagine that I could, but he was in such a state of humility in regard to his own unworthiness, and despondency as to ever winning the young person aforesaid, that he came to me for encouragement, simply from my own point of view and not in the least as compromising the adorable object."

Barbara's look of pleased superiority changed to one of bewilderment.

"But I do not understand in the least!" she exclaimed. "Did not John Featherstonhaugh propose to you?"

"No, dear, and I am very glad of it, for I should have been obliged to refuse him, and I would have been sorry to have given him pain."

"Then all I have to say is that he is an unprincipled man. What right had he to try to win your sympathy and pretend to be in love if he was not?"

"He has a perfect right to my sympathy, Barb, for he is very earnestly and honestly in love with you."

"With me!" Barbara turned suddenly aside, so that Saint could

A CONFIDENTIAL CONVERSATION.

not see her face, but the bunch of fox-gloves in her hand shook in all their tiny blossoms as though they were ringing a wedding-chime.

"He has loved you a long time, Barb, but he is very shy and distrustful of himself. I have learned to know him well, and, Barbara, he is a truly noble man. Can you not find it in your heart to care for him a little?"

"You woo very well," Barbara replied, without turning. "But do you know I think it would seem more real if John Featherstonhaugh told me this himself."

"He will find an opportunity to do so ere long, never fear. He went up to the Peak for that very purpose as soon as he could after he left us, only to find that you had started on this yachting trip."

"And did he mean me all the time in that letter he sent you at Vassar after our return from our first trip to Europe?"

"It has been you, and you only all the time, Barb."

Barbara laughed merrily. "How very stupid in him," she said, "It was just like a man, to beat about the bush in that way, and confuse matters by making us think that he cared for you, when he might have had his answer directly from me two years ago."

"A favorable answer, I trust, Barb."

"I did not say so. I am not accustomed to this courting by proxy. It may be the English fashion, but it is not the way we do things in America."

"I see that you are determined not to be serious, but there is another matter of which I wish to speak to you. When I confided John Featherstonhaugh's secret to Maud, she told me of your kind intentions toward me. Now you can but see what a worthless piece of property the Manor would be to me, and thanking you just the same I want you to keep it for yourself."

"That is all changed now, Saint, by the finding of a codicil which leaves the Manor to John Featherstonhaugh, provided he makes choice of a portionless bride, which he has done in deciding upon poor little me. To be sure I have not consented as yet to be the portionless bride, but that ought not in common justice to affect the matter at all."

"If it does you certainly can't be so hard-hearted as to keep him out of his inheritance."

"That is neither here nor there, as they say in legal papers, 'and further the deponent testifieth not.' What I wanted to say is this: You will not have the Manor, but the sum of money which was mentioned in aunt's will as an equivalent to it, and that you can carry with you to Germany or anywhere else."

"But if I refuse to accept even this, dear Barb?"

"Why then I presume it will remain in the funds that aunt left for charitable purposes. Come, Saint, don't refuse. Why should you be too proud to accept a trifle from me. I'll rewrite the conveyance and give half to Maud. We have always shared our things equally, you know."

"Then why do you not divide this legacy in thirds? You have left no part for yourself. Ah! you shy little puss. I see you would no longer be a portionless bride. Well, dear girl, I consent to receive this from your hand, as I have no doubt Maud will, provided you promise to put no let or hinderance in the way of John Featherstonhaugh's securing the Manor."

"What a set of conspirators we are! How do I know that he would care to have the Manor turned into a refuge for sick and poor children? And now that I have found my mission in life I am not going to give it up. No, not for twenty John Featherstonhaugh's. We shall see, all that will be decided in due time — but seriously, Saint, I am glad — happier than I can tell you for one thing. He chose me, knowing from Maud that I had given you all my little fortune, that I had nothing to bring him but myself, and not knowing that in so doing he made good his claim to the Manor, through the lost codicil. I have always believed him an honorable man, and it would have been very hard for me to have given up my faith in him."

"Maud told me that he seemed as delighted when he heard of your generosity. 'If anything could make me love her more,' he said, 'it would be this act of disinterestedness; it gives the key to her high, unselfish character.'"

"He was only describing himself," Barbara replied. "I make no admissions, no promises; but I will say just this. If any one ever unlocks the citadel," — here she lifted her wrist and shook the padlock bangle significantly, — "it will be with just such a key."

They sat quietly side by side for a few moments, then Barbara sprang up from her seat on the stile. "How we have gossiped," she exclaimed. "The sun is setting behind Farmer Brookfield's strawstacks, and here is Maud come in search of us. Can you realize that the good old days of Vassar comradeship are over, that in a short time Saint will be in Germany, Maud in America, and I left in this little English island?"

"What of that!" Maud replied, in her brusque matter-of-fact way. "We will meet again some day, and meantime we are certain that the old bond can never grow thin and snap, for we have Scripture assurance that a threefold cord is not quickly broken!"

That evening, as Saint and Maud were curtained in from the damp night, they talked together of Barbara.

"I am jealous to think that America is to lose her," Maud said. "There is more to her than to either of us. She was a little wilful and wayward at college, but she was always bright, and she has a heart made to fit a colossus. I have been impatient that she never chose a specialty of her own — she might easily have distinguished herself; but I have come to the conclusion that it is a blessed thing that she did not. We are the supremely selfish, while she makes herself a stepping-stone for every one she meets, not thinking at all of herself if only she may lift them a little higher. Was there ever another just like her?"

"I have found the type in a very old book," Saint replied, —

"'But if ye saw that which no eyes can see,
The inward beauty of her lovely spirit,
Garnished with heavenly gifts of high degree,
Much more then would ye wonder at that sight.

. . . . .

"'There dwell sweet love and constant chastity,
Unspotted faith, and comely womanhood,
Regard of honor, and mild modesty.'"

"And unselfishness," Maud added, "the sweetest grace of all."

IN THE PARK.

CHAPTER XII.

INTERCEPTED LETTERS.

IF this were a love-story instead of a story of friendship, we might tell how John Featherstonhaugh prospered in his wooing. As it is, we can only hint that Barbara was too high-spirited a girl to be easily won, even when the citadel was all in revolt in favor of the besieging army. She made the young man's task a sufficiently difficult one to convince him that American girls were not to be had simply for the asking, and to inspire him with a salutary respect, which their after relations never lessened. And Barbara's reluctance was not coquetry or a pretence of coyness, but a genuine, thoughtful deliberation.

"There is something very solemn in it," she said to Saint, "this pledging my love and faith until death doth us part, and I cannot do it suddenly, just because I happen to have liked him very much for a long time." When the decision was made it was unequivocal, and there was never afterward any hesitancy or regret.

Maud declined to accept any portion of the legacy, and Saint was prevailed upon to allow it to be placed to her account, adding, "But when I have finished my musical education, and am earning a large salary, nothing shall prevent my taking a financial interest in such of your protegés as exhibit a talent for music. The idea of a fund that should pass perpetually from one beneficiary to another, pleased Barbara. "We will draw up a paper," she said, "which, whoever receives your aid, shall sign. In it the person assisted shall agree, when able to repay the debt, to assist some one else under like conditions, and so on indefinitely."

"Until it reaches some ungrateful creature who will not, or some unfortunate who cannot, do so much for another," Mr. Atchison grumbled.

"That is not likely," Barbara replied, confidently; "Saint and I will make a judicious first selection in regard to these very matters, and we will cast our bread upon the waters confidently expecting"——

"To reap a whole bakery! Well, money has been squandered in more harmless ways, and I have nothing to say."

In point of fact, Mr. Atchison admired Barbara more than he admitted, and it was really remarkable how the funds left by Miss Atchison for the benefit of poor children grew and multiplied under his management. He was never required to make any reports, or possibly some very startling discrepancies of an unusual kind might have been discovered; for the most usurious interest could not have accounted for the income which the small principal in his trust some way contrived to yield.

The three girls continued their confidential relations after seas separated them, and each found herself the busy centre of friends and responsibilities in widely differing associations. Indeed, they were never as free in conversations with others as in the thick-folded, many-stamped letters which the mail-steamers carried for them between the continents. Robbing the mails is not to be commended in actual life, but the crime within the covers of a story is not heavily punished, and from these letters we can best obtain a picture of their daily life.

Barbara wrote to Saint respecting hers, as follows: —

"You should see the Manor since uncle has added the new wing for the children. Mother Featherstonhaugh is as much interested in our plan as any of us; but uncle thought best that the old home-life of the Manor should not be encroached upon. An addition has been thrown out on the lawn-tennis ground, under the shade of the mag-

KENSINGTON GARDENS.

nificent old elms and beeches, which you always said resembled those of Kensington Gardens. John designed the wing, so that it is in perfect keeping with the rest of the mansion. The windows are latticed with diamond panes, and look out on the trimly clipped box-hedges which are Jim's pride and one of the family heirlooms, for they were set out by Gladys' grandfather, and are equal in beauty to any that we saw in the old cloister-gardens of Spain and Portugal.

"I have an able corps of assistants: one trained nurse, a kindergarten teacher, two maids, and Joe, who is general factotum, and a great comfort. Just now we have eight guests. One is a little girl who is suffering with spinal complaint, and will probably remain with us permanently. Another is an Italian violinist, who was taken away from some street musicians, who ill-treated him, and who belongs to the little class that recite regularly to me (I fancy he will pass from my hands to yours one of these days). Two sisters are here only for rest and recreation, and will return to the factory in cool weather. One bright boy, who has been going to the bad, Joe and I am trying to teach to speak the truth. When we feel that we can trust him, there is a situation ready, but he does not know it. Four children, three of them little tots, whose mother has been recently left a penniless widow, but can support herself if the children are cared for, make up the number.

"Mrs. Isham visited us the other day with Tina, whom she persists in calling a member of my first graduating class. Both of Tina's foster-parents are devotedly attached to her, and she is really a very lovable child. She brought with her some dolls, which she had dressed very prettily for our nursery.

"Gladys is a dear sister, and is continually running in to borrow some of the children for a drive, or to announce some new plan for our pleasure. Tom sent us an exquisite dinner-service of Royal Worcester ware as a wedding present. I think that Gladys and he will be married at Christmas, and that they will spend their winters at Worcester, since the old reason for delay no longer exists, as it will be only a pleasure for me to have Mother Featherstonhaugh moved in her wheeled-chair to our side of the house.

"You must not think of me as a prisoner here, with my hobby. John's work takes him to many cathedral towns, gay watering-places, fine old estates, and sometimes to London; and I have already been away with him on two such trips, Gladys taking my place here. One of these gave me a delightful week at Lincoln, where I had my first introduction to a real English cathedral. Next to York, this is John's favorite. Its two western towers rise gracefully and aspiringly skyward; while the grand central tower, three hundred feet from foot to pinnacle, reminded me, in its majesty, of a noble soul, firm, unmovable, and lifted above the petty things of sordid, everyday life. John says my simile is all wrong, for the noblest souls are those who stoop to the lowest and meanest. There is a glorious rose-window in the north transept; and the angel choir, with its sculptured seraphs, is a beautiful conceit. I spent a part of each day in the wonderful place, until my neck was awry with gazing at the wonderful wood-carving and stone vaulting. I grew to have a friendly feeling for the hideous old monuments, even; and I bade good-by to the effigies of Catharine, wife of John of Gaunt, and to Joan, Countess of Westmoreland, as though they were old acquaintances.

GARGOYLE.

The Galilee Porch, the Easter Sepulchre, and the Lady Chapel, had each their fascination for me; and the grotesque gargoyles and corbels, as they leered upon me from under the eaves, gave me a cer-

LINCOLN CATHEDRAL.

tain satisfaction as well, for what harm could come to one within walls that had power to turn the demons to stone? I think it must have been from gargoyles such as these that Jean Ingelow caught her fancy of the curate walking in the old minster, and overhearing the talk of the evil spirits as they complained of him, and —

'Such as haunt the yawning mouths of hell,
And pluck them back that run thereto.'

"It was a comforting lesson that the evil ones were permitted to teach the disheartened curate, that even poverty and death were God's angels. Do you remember how one of the demons snarled to the other, 'We do, and we delight to do our best.' But that is little, —

'If we grudge and snatch away the bread,
Then will He save by poverty, and gain
By early giving up of blameless life.'

"It is good for us workers to reflect occasionally that when we fail in some part of what we would have liked to accomplish, that it is because the Master Workman has given that particular task to abler agencies than ours: —

'We are not bound to make all wrong go right,
But only to discover, and to do
With cheerful heart the work that God appoints.'

"I am more than ever enchanted with this rich old England, the more I see of it; and I am thankful that it still holds so many surprises for me, enough for a lifetime, if I do not devour the country at one gulp, as our tourists sometimes do. Father is coming over next summer, and we mean to make an excursion through the Lake country in phætons. We shall visit Windermere, Grasmere, and the delightful haunts of Southey, Wordsworth, and De Quincy. Can you not come over and join us?

"Your life in Weimar must be very delightful. It is certainly a privilege to be the pupil of such a man as Liszt. I was glad to hear that the Germans have such a good opinion of American girls. I presume it is because the many Germans in America send back a good account of us. How strange it is that the English, with whom we are so 'more than kin,' should be 'so less than kind.' But the barriers are breaking, and perhaps they would never have existed if we could have kept some mannerless specimens of young America, of whom we are all ashamed, in their native country until they had acquired a trifle more of good sense and good taste. We Vassar girls, at least, cannot complain of any lack of cordiality in the treatment which we have received. I met Lord Gubbins at uncle's not long since, and he had much to say about you. He had always considered Gladys Featherstonhaugh the neatest specimen of what could be done in the way of a young woman, but really he was inclined now to yield the palm to that young person from *the other* Chelsea. It was a great pity that she would n't let him take her to the Ascot, — American girls had such odd ideas about racing not being in good form, etc., etc.

"Did you know that Mr. Ruskin has paid an American girl twenty-five hundred dollars for a hand-illustrated book of Italian stories? In one of his lectures at Oxford, he said, 'I would fain have said an English girl, but all my prejudices have lately had the axe laid to their roots, one by one; she is an American!' If autocratic Mr. Ruskin can recant as honestly as this, his dictum that no true art can come out of America, the genuine opinion of the English public will change as generously as soon as it knows us better.

"It is time for me to give the oldest of my girls a lesson in bookkeeping; she has a talent for business, and Lady Gubbins has offered to start her in a thread and needle store.

"I enclose Maud's last letter. It is too good to be wasted alone on

"Yours, lovingly,   BARB."

"NEW YORK, Feb.

'DEAREST BARB,— The latest occurrence with us, in which you are likely to be interested, is doubtless the annual meeting of the Alumnæ, which took place last week at Delmonico's, and as you could not be there, as was your right, I want to tell you all about it. To me it seemed an unusually pleasant occasion; but perhaps that is only because I enjoy each meeting more as it whirls around. I wonder who originated the idea, it was such a happy one, for the graduates of Vassar, who find themselves in New York or its vicinity at this time of the year, to meet and spend a social afternoon with one another. That Alumnæ Association is more to us than Masonic Fraternity or Army League, or Guild, or Club, can be to the masculine half of humanity.

"Its confessed object — to keep alive an interest in our Alma Mater — is the least of its results. I have failed to meet the graduate who needed to have her interest quickened; but the ostensible purpose makes a rallying cry which appeals to us all, and brings us together when nothing else would. It resurrects dead friendships, brings girls in fashionable life who are in danger of forgetting the old traditions, and of frittering away their being upon society into contact with earnest students and workers who need to drop their hobbies for a time and learn a lesson in rest and recreation. The girls are interested in and influence one another in a very salutary way; struggling merit meets social recognition, lethargic minds are stimulated, selfish hearts warmed, solitary souls gladdened. It is like a church, and better, unless maybe a church under the influence of one of the old-fashioned revivals, where every meeting was a love feast, and the word sister meant something more than cant. You may think that I am exaggerating the effect of a meeting which occurs only once a year; but the contact does not cease on that one day. I saw Mrs. Arthur Livingston (you'll remember her better, perhaps, as Belle Lovejoy) taking Ellen Smith home in her carriage. Ellen is teaching in the public schools, and has a patient but hopeless look which is sad to see. Belle was asking her advice about some new entertainment for her four o'clock teas, and Ellen suggested literary readings. Belle was delighted, and asked her to give the first one, and submit a plan for them to act upon in future. It will be an excellent thing for both of them.

"You should have seen how we girls chattered, — for seeing would have been more comfortable than hearing; and girls we all are. Even the antediluvians who graduated away back in '69, and confess to thirty years and over, are as young at heart as any of us, though they may be mothers of families or learned specialists in science. We had an essay, reports from committees, a lunch that was not to be despised, and we *talked!* I believe I will give you a hodge-podge of what I heard. I happened at first to get stranded in the dressing-room in a set that belonged to a different dynasty from the one in which I flourished. I sat quietly after the maid had fitted on my slippers, and tried to boil down everything I heard, and make an analysis of the residuum, feeling that in this way I would arrive at a fair estimate of an alumna. The result reminds me of one of the crazy quilts that old ladies are so fond of patching. While vividly startling in spots the general effect was not homogeneous. I did not always hear an entire sentence, remarks overlapped each other, and now and then a quiet, humdrum conversation had an exclamation projected into it like a bombshell from some one at quite a distance. It was something like this —

"'Marion Beach!' 'Yes, Marion Beach Oakley, I've taken another degree, you know, I '— 'discovered an asteroid in the constellation of' 'the Society for Ethical Culture, and' 'went as a missionary, says she likes Japan almost as much as' 'your charming musicales. How did you induce Gerster to sing for you? I thought she never' 'wrote a work on Protoplasm that the savants all say upsets the generally received' 'school for Apache and Comanche

IN THE DRESSING-ROOM.

children, it is really touching to see how devoted they are to ' ' birds, breasts and tutts fruth,' 'really the most *recherche* little entertainment since' 'Margaret Sterling's lecture on the Abolition of the Death Penalty, Senator Stockstill said that he should not be surprised if every member of Congress voted for' 'æsthetic dresses of olive green Madras lace, with peacock fans attached to' 'the surgeon of the Woman's Hospital had a very critical case submitted to her of a young woman who' 'was admitted to the bar with her husband, but passed the better examination of the two, before I'd marry a man beneath the level of' 'deep-sea sounding, resulting in the discovery of ever so many new species of marine algæ, some of them ' ' working in prisons like a regular Mrs. Elizabeth Fry. She reports one apparently abandoned creature, who was sentenced for life for' 'studying theology and has already had a pastorate offered her as the associate of' 'the fashion editor of' 'a scientific expedition to South America to collect specimens for ' 'a work on abstruse mathematics' 'which Joseffy played at his farewell concert, the most entrancing thing, and every one was electrified when it finally crept out that it was composed by' 'a specialist in diphtheria and throat troubles. Lily Lawrence sent for her when her baby had the croup. Lily's husband thought that she ought not to have chosen her just because she happened to be a classmate, and had no faith whatever in her ability, but before Annie left the house the infant' 'translated Herculano's History of Portugal in ten volumes' 'and succeeds wonderfully as an architect, designing the best set of apartment houses which have ever been put up in New York, with a fire-escape from each floor leading directly to' — 'the centre of Abyssinia.'

"After a time I slipped away to a window alcove, where I saw some of our class. They were all wild to hear about you. 'You can tell me what you please about her,' Clara Carter said, 'I shall not be in the least surprised. I could credit the most remarkable or startling information; Barbara Atchison was capable of anything.'

When I told them that you had married an Englishman, and were living in a charming manor-house in Derbyshire, they said that was all very nice and romantic, but not at all up to what one might have expected from Barb. Vassar girls are a little *exigeantes*, even after graduation, you see. Only the very highest success, or a magnificent failure will satisfy them — mediocrity is the one unpardonable sin. However, I did surprise them; for when I said your home was filled with factory children from Manchester, whom you petted, nursed, taught, and encouraged, as they most needed — though Clara had assured me that she believed you could do anything, they insisted that I was joking, and refused to credit it. 'If you had told me that she had gone upon the stage, or taken the veil, as a nun, I could have believed it,' Clara said; 'she was a girl of extremes, but quiet, persistent; self-sacrifice was not in her line.' 'I don't think Barb considers it sacrifice,' I replied, 'and 'I don't think any of us quite knew her in the old days.' Then we fell to discussing all the old girls, and it transpired that almost every one surprised us by what she had done or failed to do.

"Dashing Nell Delano, who was such a cut-up that she barely escaped being sent home, married a minister, and is very popular with her husband's congregation, teaching the young men's Bible class, and an enthusiastic worker in the cause of home missionsr Little, shrinking, sensitive Violet Fairchild is a surgeon, noted for her nerve and decision in difficult cases. Indolent Lolla Fanning writes a story every week for one of the city newspapers. It seems that no one thought that Saint was particularly talented; and when they heard that she had composed a sonata, which Liszt had praised, and to which he had written a prelude, they were all electrified. Myra Carter made an observation which seemed to me very just, but which had never struck me before. She thought that one great benefit which we received at Vassar was a development of latent energies, whose existence we never suspected, and a pruning of individual

AN ENGLISH CHURCHYARD.

extravagances. This levelling process, which occurs naturally where many young people associate together, comes first. The shy are encouraged to self-confidence by seeing it in others; the over-bold are shamed into reticence; the meek gain in spirit; the enthusiastic are toned down; the nervous are calmed; the apathetic are stimulated. Then when the Vassar mint has given its common stamp to us, and we are all turned out, freshly polished, and as alike in outward seeming as two coins from the same mould, we begin to knock about the world, and our native metal gives its characteristic ring. The bronze for strength and the gold for value, and we find that what we have lost in the refining and minting process is only individual dross, while the individual metal has gained in quality.

"And now what of myself? I have nothing very astonishing to report. I have a cozy little studio which looks out on Broadway from the top of the Vienna Bakery Building, with the chimes of Grace Church on my right hand, and the great marble vanity fair, that was once Stewart's store, on my left. Across the way, Bunnell's Museum displays its gaudy posters, depicting the bearded lady and the tattooed man; from beneath, come savory sniffs of buns and rolls; and far down, like a stream at the foot of my cliff, Broadway brawls and surges. Here I sit in a closet of a room and decorate plaques and tea-cups. It is not a very lofty ideal, is it? But I have this consolation: I never could have made a great artist if I had devoted my entire life to the attempt, and I am a good designer and decorator. Long before I had any idea that I should need to support myself, I recognized the fact that what little talent I possessed was of the merchantable order, and I determined to perfect this lower gift instead of straining after the unattainable. Now I have the satisfaction of knowing that I could not have spent my time more profitably if I had known what was coming. I see so many heart-rending instances of failure in this city,—young girls trying to support themselves in art by decorating boxes and fans, menus, and Easter-cards *poorly;* and failing just because they have only half-learned their profession, and the things produced are not really good. The market is overstocked with cheap decoration; the public no longer demand that grade of work; it has grown critical and discriminating. People say that the rage for decoration is passing, but skilled work still commands high prices; and if I have been fortunate I can say without egotism it is because I have deserved it by a painstaking preparation for just this adaptation of art. I have a fine position as designer for a porcelain manufactory, and do other outside work. Mother is in Florida this winter with father, who has been suffering with nervous prostration ever since his business affairs took their bad turn. He is improving, however, and it seems that one great cause of his worry was the thought that I would not be able to support myself. Now that he sees how finely I am succeeding, so that I can even help him and mamma to such little luxuries as this trip South, his spirits have greatly improved. They think in the spring of going out to Europe to join my sister Lily. I shall be quite alone then, — perhaps not more so than I am now; but at present I have their letters, and the necessity and pleasure of looking out for them, and seeing to it that little checks leave and are received regularly. It will seem quite desolate to have to provide only for one's self.

"This is already such a letter in length as only we three write; but I must tell you of an adventure I had with a burglar the other night, and how it unexpectedly brought me face to face with your Cousin Dick. Don't be alarmed, my dear. Dick was not the burglar.

"After the Alumnæ lunch at Delmonico's, Edith Richland insisted on my going home with her; and as there was really no reason for my not doing so, and Edith was to be alone that evening, — her husband had gone to Washington on business, — I went. We were chatting together in the parlor, and had not lighted the gas when we heard a step in the room overhead. Edith flew upstairs, fancying that her mother-in-law, Madam Richland, might need her. I sat by the window, looking across the moonlit snow to the quiet park, and thinking what a pretty effect it would be to paint. Suddenly Edith shrieked, and I noticed the figure of a man climbing down the rose trellis which connects the upper and lower balcony. I ran to the front door and caught hold of his knees. He could not let go his grip of the trellis for fear of falling, and I had him fast; but he kicked disagreeably, and I knew that I could not hold him long. Edith screamed Help! police! and fire! but the avenue was as deserted and silent as a street in Pompeii. Presently the butler came creeping cautiously up from the area, and seeing how I was occupied, offered to go for a policeman, and acted upon his own suggestion with the utmost alacrity. Then we were entirely alone, and the burglar, tired of the situation loosened his hold, and came crashing to the ground. He scrambled to his feet, and would have escaped, but at that instant a young man crossed the street from the Park, and attracted by Edith's cries hurried to us. He had been skating, and reaching us just as our burglar started to run he clubbed him with the skates, and felled him once more to the sidewalk, where he knelt on his breast, pinioning him to the earth, and holding him until the policeman arrived and took his prisoner in charge. There was something very familiar in the outline of the stranger's head, with its boyish polo cap, as he held the prostrate burglar, the moonlight reflected upon their faces, and their figures sharply dark against the snow; but when the policeman appeared and he sprang to his feet with a bow to us, I saw that it was Dick Atchison. Edith came down the steps and invited him in; he was declining politely when I added an invitation, and really a more astonished face I never saw.

"'I thought you might be in New York,' he said, 'but I could not find your name in the directory.'

" He is in town attending to business connected with his mills in Alabama, which promise very well. Was it not odd that he should have happened upon us so opportunely. He has improved wonderfully, and already makes a very good American. It seems very natural to me for people to come to us from every nation, but that you should give up your country as you have done, I cannot quite forgive. We lose too much, and I am going to contrive some way to tempt John Featherstonhaugh to emigrate.

"Good-by, dear heart; write me when you've no more pressing charity at your hand. Life has given you the sweetest privilege of all, — that of helping others. If it ever comes in my reach, you may be sure that I shall luxuriate in it; at present, perhaps, all that I can bear is the delight of helping myself.

"Through the past, the present, and future,

"Faithfully yours, MAUD."

Saint wrote from Germany: —

"BELOVED MAUD, — It seems very odd to be studying here without you. I turn from the piano involuntarily to ask you how you like that movement, and often fancy that I detect the odor of turpentine and hear you cleaning your brushes.

"You wrote to Barb of the pleasure of helping others, and of helping yourself. Do you know there is an humble joy in being aided as I am? It seems to me that every one extends largess to me, and that I am bankrupt in purse and heart. To you first, then to Barb, and now to Herr Liszt. My mission seems to be now to absorb; perhaps by and by I shall be of better use than merely to bring out the good graces of others. Life is so short and art is long, I wonder whether I shall ever accomplish what I wish. Herr Liszt feels that he has only begun; and so many great artists have died, saying that they had only learned the technique of their art, had spent their lives in finding out *how* to express themselves without expressing anything. You know what Omar says of life: —

GOETHE'S PROMENADE, WEIMER.

> "'Tis but a tent where takes his one day's rest,
> A sultan to the realm of Death addressed,
> The sultan rises, and the dark farrash
> Strikes and prepares it for another guest.
> A moment's halt, a momentary taste
> Of being from the well amid the waste,
> And lo! the phantom caravan has reached
> The nothing it set out from. Oh! make haste!'

"This frightens me; more than this, it would palsy every effort if I believed the last line, for death is swifter than human endeavor, and all haste would be useless if the tasks begun and unfinished here are always left as fragments. I prefer, while hasting, to think with Browning —

> 'No matter, what's come to perfection perishes,
> Work begun upon earth we shall finish in Heaven.'

"I wrote you so recently of our life at Weimar, and each day follows so exactly in the footsteps of the preceding, that you will not expect any description of place or relation of incident. I am consumed with a student's enthusiasm, — there is no delight like it! I played Herr Liszt's *Chant d'Amour* for him the other evening, and he gratified me with many kind commendations. He made me sing '*Du bist wie eine Blume*,' and assured me that I had a native feeling for expression, both through the medium of voice and touch. What an ecstacy there is in struggle and achievement? I am glad that we never fully succeed, — that new heights stretch on beyond; it is this thought that reconciles me to eternity.

"And now you will pretend to be jealous, and will say that I care more for my work than for the old friendship; but while you say such things you well know in your heart of hearts that they are not true; that Vassar has twisted our threefold cord so tightly that the strands can never fall apart.

"That was a pretty conceit of Barb's beneficiary, Cutery Joe, to make her husband a wedding-present of a scarf-pin in the shape of a key, which should exactly fit the little padlock which he made for her on their yachting cruise, and with which she promised to lock her heart. The boy has more wit than his appearance would indicate; but really, don't you think, dear Maud, that you and I ought to have duplicate keys?"

www.ingramcontent.com/pod-product-compliance
Lightning Source LLC
Chambersburg PA
CBHW021816230426
43669CB00008B/767